MY STRETCH IN ALTCOURSE PRISON.

PART TWO.

When I published my first book about Altcourse Prison there were some surprising and interesting spin-offs. The North Wales Daily Post published a full, two-page spread about this book. In it, I described the Vampire Killer. This was a seventeen years old boy who ripped the heart out of an 82 years old lady and then drank her blood in the belief that he would become a vampire and live forever. (He was mistaken.) In early 2018 I was contacted by Monster Films who were making a series of documentaries entitled, 'Murder by the Sea?' I was interviewed on television about this same lad, and again, I received a lot of attention from various people. I was later contacted by the same movie people who were filming a documentary about an unpleasant, young man named Mitchell Quy. This fellow murdered his wife in conditions of extreme brutality, cut her body up into little bits with an angle grinder, and then buried the pieces in different locations all round Southport. Nice guy!

One of the more intelligent critiques I received about my first prison book suggested that I should continue at more length and in greater detail with my chapter entitled, 'Jail Stories.'

I decided to accept this suggestion.

I would like to express my sincere thanks to all the people who took the time and trouble to make intelligent and positive critiques about the books I have written.

SOME INTERESTING CASES!

THE BUTCHER.

THE LADY KILLER.

THE GANGSTER.

THE FOOL.

THE LIAR.

THE SOLDIER.

THE SAILOR.

THE COPPER.

THE SCREW.

THE DOCTOR.

THE NURSE.

THE IRISHMAN.

THE ULSTERMAN.

THE LADY.

THE GENTLEMAN.

THE NONCE.

THE GRASS.

THE MURDERER.

THE JUNKIE.

THE PSYCHOPATH.

THE BANKER.

THE STUDENT.

THE ACTOR.

THE ARTIST.

THE VEGETARIAN.

THE IDIOT.

THE DINOSAUR.

THE OVERDOSE.

THE TRAMP.

THE BIG FELLAH.

THE FIRST TIMER.

THE PAD THIEF.

THE RUGBY PLAYER.

MY FIRST EVER, FIRST RESPONSE!

TRANSFER TO A MENTAL HOSPITAL.

THE GOOD SAMARITANS.

TWENTY-EIGHT DAYS.

A FUNNY STORY.

A SAD STORY.

AN UNPLEASANT STORY.

THE LITTLE GIRL.

THE SELF HARMER.

THE DIRTY PROTEST.

THE DRINK OF WATER.

FOUR MILLION POUNDS.

BURIED BODIES.

A RATHER UNUSUAL PROTEST.

'YOU CAN'T TAKE THIS OFF ME.'

RACIAL PREJUDICE IN PRISONS.

METHADONE. A PERSONAL OPINION.

PLUGGING.

THE TELEPHONE CALL.

THE TURNSTILE.

THE SHOOTING MAN.

ONE BIG LAD.

THE BUTCHER.

I met Mitchell Quy on Reynoldstown Blue which is the Rule 43 Wing in

Altcourse Prison. This is the NONCES wing. (Not of Normal Criminal

Element.) These are men whose profession or crime (for instance a policeman or sex offender) makes them unacceptable to the general prison population who

are the O.D.Cs. (Ordinary Decent Criminals.) This Wing is also known as the

VP wing. (Vulnerable Prisoners.) Under Rule 43 the Governor or Prison

Director can remove an inmate from ordinary prison population on the grounds

of 'good order and discipline.' If he himself is under threat for instance, or may

be a threat to other prisoners or staff.' He fulfilled these conditions admirably.

Mitchell Quy was one of the many unpleasant psychopaths I met during my,

prison career. He approached me on the Wing and asked. 'Do you know who I

am?'

My answer was. 'No.'

I always denied knowing who a criminal was. If you admit knowing about him, you give him a sense of his own self-importance and inflate his ego. Quy was

married to a beautiful, young lady who mysteriously disappeared. He insisted

that she had run off with another man. He even appeared on television stating

that he wanted her back and protesting his love for her. Quy gave an interview

with the Liverpool Echo which it later transpired was, 'a tissue of lies.' He even

faked a letter which he claimed to have received from a woman which claimed

that, 'my husband has run off with your wife.'

This was more lies.

Like many psychopaths Quy loved being the centre of attention and he

described to me how he had appeared on television when questioned about his wife's disappearance. He obviously believed himself to be a celebrity. Before

the murder trial he was also sentenced for passing dud cheques. He complained

bitterly of being threatened with death because people thought he had murdered

his wife. He was very indignant about this. It was then proved that he had

murdered his wife. He strangled the poor girl in the bath. When describing this

to me Quy told me that, as he choked her, he noticed one, single, lone tear

dribbling down her cheek as he killed her. This made him feel guilty and cruel,

he claimed. But he continued to strangle her until she was dead. He then

asked his brother to help him dispose of it. They cut the body into small pieces,

placed the bits in carrier bags and bin liners and buried the pieces in various locations around Southport. Her hands and head were never found. He was

remanded to Altcourse Jail.

V.P.s tend to fall into two very distinct types. There is the snivelling,

whingeing, whining types and the arrogant, bragging, boasting ones. Mitchell

Quy was the arrogant sort. He was placed on the VP Wing both because

of the brutality of his crime and because of his unpleasant personality which

made him unpopular with other prisoners.

This man had a behaviour pattern of psychopaths who have committed some

form of heinous crime. Quy was true to this pattern. On several occasions he

told me emphatically. 'No one has any sympathy for me.' In this instance he

was correct. No one did have any sympathy for him.

Quy had the classic personality traits of the aggressive psychopath. During

one conversation with me he told me that he had buried his wife's liver under a

bridge in Southport. Then he laughed out loud and commented. 'Do you get it?

'The Bridge over the liver of Quy.' (The Bridge over the River of Kwai!)

He thought this was a joke.

No! I did not laugh.

Like many psychopaths he always laughed at bad news, and other people's

misfortunes. Whether or not the bad luck was to a friend or an enemy was

irrelevant. There is a German word, schadenfreude, which literally translated

means, 'joy in harm'. A colloquial translation means, taking joy from the

misfortunes or harm of others. Psychopaths, tend to burst out laughing at bad news, whether the misfortune is that of a friend or an enemy. The

psychopath is extremely impulsive and may be prone to outbursts of violence.

They are emotionally demanding in the extreme and rarely give anything in

return. They are incapable of any real emotional attachment to others. They

display cunning, manipulation, grandiosity, superficial charm, callousness and

impulsivity. They are very convincing and when they are in a good mood,

they may put an act on during which they dupe people into believing their lies.

They even seem to believe the lies themselves. They project themselves as the

victim rather than the criminal. They show a glaring lack of remorse, feeling,

insight, foresight, duty, loyalty, empathy, responsibility or any other emotion.

Sometimes they do not even have self-pity.

Mind you Quy himself, had plenty of self-pity. Many psychopaths display a

condition known as grandiosity. This is a personality trait in which, quite

simply, the person believes that are a great deal more important than they

really are. Quy laughed as he told me how he had sent a Christmas Present to

the senior Police Officer investigating his wife's disappearance. The present

was a bottle of black hair dye because he, 'felt sorry,' for the man as his hair

was turning grey. In all seriousness I doubt if Mitchell Quy ever felt sorry for

any other human being in his entire life. Even the trial Judge later commented

on his, 'breath-taking cynicism.'

On the day after he was sentenced, he approached me on the wing. I was dispensing medication through a steel barred gate. He asked me eagerly. 'Did

you see me on television last night?'

I replied, 'No. I did not. 'Even if I had seen it, I would always reply, 'No.'

If you agree that you saw him on television, then again, you are reinforcing his

negative personality and behaviour.

He seemed very disappointed. He expected that everyone the prison would now

recognise his star status and he also expected to be treated as the celebrity that

he felt he was. He was very upset that this did not happen.

As I left the Wing, he stopped me. 'What happens now?' he asked.

He seemed genuinely curious.

I grinned. This is common behaviour with psychopaths. There are eight

Category Triple 'A' prisons in Britain. 'What happens now?'' is that an

offender such as this is shipped to one of them. He is then in a High Security

Wing full off equally unpleasant and psychopathic prisoners who all believe

that each one of them is 'special,' in some way. And every single man will be

serving a long sentence and every one of them will claim celebrity status

because of the heinous nature of his crimes. They even have arguments with

each other about who has committed the most, evil crimes.

When I took a moment or two to explain all of this to Quy he seemed rather

nonplussed and disappointed. As with many such men reality was starting to

sink in. He was even starting to lose the inane smile with which his face was normally plastered.

A couple of days later Quy took an overdose of the anti-depressants that he had

been prescribed before the trial. He had saved these tablets up over a period of

weeks. Inmates are supposed to have their mouths checked to see if they have

swallowed their medication. This sounds great in theory. As always, reality is

different. A nurse dispenses medication through the inch-thick, steel bars of a

gated door. There should be a prison officer there to keep order and to help

check that the prisoner has swallowed the tablets. Frequently there is not. In

Altcourse Prison there were plenty of times when two officers, who might well

be young girls in their twenties, would be left to control an entire wing of perhaps seventy male inmates. If a nurse is dispensing medication on a busy day

and a line-up of twenty or thirty men are taking it in turn to be served, and many

of them have all sorts of different requests and questions for which they each

demand an instant response then completing a medication round properly can be

difficult to say the least. There is always the odd idiot who will take pleasure in

being as disruptive as possible. They may well ask awkward questions for

instance, demand a sick note to excuse them from work, ask for a doctor's

appointment and make other requests. Then there is the inmate who will make

play the fool. All of this makes it difficult for any nurse to be as vigilant as they

should be when dispensing tablets and makes it possible for inmates to secrete medication.

In jail 'pills' are currency. They can be sold, swapped, given, lent or bartered

for coffee, tea, tobacco, sugar, sweets, dirty magazines, a blow job, toothpaste,

shampoo or after-shave. Many inmates save up their tablets and then take a

large amount all at one time to get a 'high,' or a 'low' off the bigger amount.

We live in a pill culture and many people outside and inside of jail demand

tablets for totally inappropriate reasons. Doctors and nurses, both in and out of

jail often face completely impractical requests. People approach them

with sad stories, 'my wife is unfaithful to me,' 'I am unemployed,' 'my son is a

drug addict,' and much more. Often what they ask for is something that the doctor simply cannot give. In the end many doctors give them medication

simply to get rid of them. It is also a strange anomaly that when people really

are depressed and genuinely attempt suicide they invariably swallow the tablets

that are the ones that are available.

And trycyclic anti-depressants are quite lethal.

Quy was lucky.

He did not die.

He was shipped to a long-stay, high-security Jail.

I hope he likes it there.

THE LADY KILLER.

(DEATH ON THE NILE.)

I had two main jobs as a Psychiatric Nurse in Altcourse Jail. My first job was the Admission of new inmates. On arrival every man was seen by a Registered Mental Nurse and had a mental, social and physical assessment. Sometimes he had a simple problem which a nurse could treat. A cut or wound for instance, which required a dressing. Other problems might need specialist care. In such case the man could then be referred on, at the nurse's discretion or the inmate's request. Many inmates ask for a detoxification regime because they claim to be rattling (withdrawing) off drugs and these are the most troublesome of prisoners. They make unrealistic requests which cannot conceivably be met, allied to a litany of threats and complaints when these demands are refused. And when they are prescribed some medication or other, they always protest that they need, 'more tablets,' 'better tablets,' 'stronger tablets.' Other inmates request an alcohol withdrawal regime, and these men are a dream in comparison. Admissions were my speciality in Altcourse Jail which was one reason why I met so many interesting cases.

Many prisoners were listed for R.M.N. follow up. There might be a history of mental illness, perhaps coupled with suicide attempts and/or self- harm. Sometimes a man would be referred simply because of the serious nature of his offences. There is a commonly held, but erroneous belief, that when a person has committed an evil, serious crime he must be insane. People will state. 'He must be mad to do something like that.' This is rubbish. In the Second World War thousands of people staffed the Concentration Camps and committed the most appalling atrocities imaginable. And no one! Not any of the defending lawyers! None of prosecuting Allied Nations! Not even the Nazis themselves! No one, ever suggested that they were, 'mentally ill.' In fact, when Camp guards were interviewed by psychiatrists after the War the fact that came across most strongly was that they were just ordinary people who had been propelled by extraordinary circumstances into extraordinary actions.

This does not make them any less guilty. We all have free will.

My second job was to visit inmates on the wings at the request of a staff member. This might be a doctor, nurse, prison officer or anyone else who wanted a psychiatric opinion. I met John Allan when he was remanded to Altcourse Jail charged with an horrific murder. He was referred to see an R.M.N. in order to assess his mental state. The R.M.N. would recommend any planned future action for the inmate. He might to see the prison doctor, to be referred for counselling, be advised to go to the gym. He might need to see a psychiatrist. Numerous possibilities. He might even need medication.

Allan was located on Canal wing which was the Category 'A' wing for dangerous criminals.

There are three categories of grade 'A' status. These are Single 'A', double 'A' and Triple 'A.' Allan was on Canal because he was a Single 'A.' Many people find it amazing that a man accused of such serious crimes was graded as a single 'A.' There are good reasons for this.

A man who is Triple 'A' is, 'a senior member of a large, dangerous gang which has access to firearms and/or explosives and would be prepared to use violence to free him.' Such a man would be a big gangster or perhaps a member of a violent, well-disciplined society such as Al-Qaeda or the Mafia. There are less than seventy Triple 'A' prisoners in British prisons so that works out at about one Cat Triple 'A' prisoner per million of the population. Obviously, this is the highest classification.

Clearly a man like Allan did not conform to these criteria. He was a Single 'A,' category.' This classification is, 'a person whose escape would be injurious to National Security and/or public safety but would be considered unlikely to have outside help.'

I inquired for Allan at the wing console. I always preferred to see men in the dining area. There are numerous well-spaced tables and chairs which allow privacy. If trouble erupts there are plenty of witness's and, in case of violence, there are prison officers nearby. 'Hello,' I introduced myself. 'My name is Chris. I am one of the Psychiatric

Nurses in this prison. Basically, I see new men in Admissions. I also interview lads who have never been in jail before. Or men charged with serious offences. I have been asked to have a word with you. How are you? How are you settling in? Are you getting on with the officers alright? Are you getting on with the lads alright?' These are open-ended questions which nearly always elicit answers and initiate a conversation.

'Nice to meet you,' he replied as he sat facing me.

Many a time I have heard lurid stories from various people about how they met some notorious killer or other and when they, 'looked into his eyes' they could, 'see pure evil.' This is rubbish. In thirty-eight years of Mental Nursing I can count on the fingers of one hand the number of times I felt this.

Usually the people who relate such a yarn have met one murderer.

Perhaps once!

Unlike most people I have personally met literally hundreds of murderers.

Hundreds of times!

But it makes a good story.

On first meeting John Allan appeared to be a perfectly ordinary sort of chap. He was a well-built, softly, spoken, middle-aged man. He had an aura of superficial, but unconvincing, charm. Beneath the surface he had the kind of underlying arrogance and grandiosity that is the hallmark of the psychopath. The conversation was, at first, very superficial.

When an R.M.N. is interviewing people, it is essential to win their confidence and get them talking. A good technique to achieve rapport is to introduce some totally neutral subject into the conversation. The golden rule is that it must be something which the patient, or inmate, is interested in. It is no good talking about football to someone who hates sport. I started out with a simple question. 'Where are you from?' He lived in Birkenhead. I know that town well and we chatted for some minutes. 'What do you do in your spare time?' I asked casually.

He looked at me in some surprise. 'I play golf,' he answered quietly. 'Are you a player?'

'No,' I replied. 'It's something I've never tried.'

Again, he looked straight at me. 'What do you do in your spare time?' he inquired.

I have tried numerous hobbies and occupations in my life, but my main interest has always been guns and shooting. For obvious reasons I never discussed this with inmates. 'I like sailing,' I answered truthfully. I guessed that this would stimulate a reply.

He seemed interested. 'Sounds great,' he replied. 'What kind of boat do you have?'

'I had a twenty-foot cabin cruiser,' I replied.

We chatted about boats for a few minutes. Then the conversation turned back to golf. 'You should take up golf,' enthused Allan. 'It's great way to meet nice ladies.'

I looked at him thoughtfully. 'I'll bear that in mind,' I replied.

'Are you married?' he asked me.

'No,' I'm divorced,' I answered truthfully. At the time my last wife had left me, so this was a true answer. (Although I was widowed before this marriage.)

As a rule of thumb, it is good policy to refrain from telling lies when talking to inmates, although sometimes it is impossible to be totally truthful.

'If you want to meet wealthy women,' he elaborated. 'Golf clubs are the place. And the women there are all really fit. Golf is great exercise.' By now the conversation was becoming more and more relaxed.

We continued talking. 'What are you charged with?' I inquired casually. In prison most inmates want to talk about their crimes, whether they claim guilt or innocence. Allan explained that he was charged with murder. 'It was all a tragic accident,' he explained. 'A lady I knew died accidentally. But the evidence against me is all a load of rubbish,' he stated emphatically. 'It's all a mistake. I will be free soon.'

I don't think he realised, at that time, exactly how strong the case was against him. The accident had happened in Egypt. I explained that I have travelled all over Africa and we started chatting about the Black Continent. This all worked! He was talking. When you do this, as a Mental Nurse you are not just passing the time. In fact, you must be careful that you do not give away too much of your own life. But when you have a conversation going between two people it is far more difficult than most people realise for the inmate to refrain from giving away his own personality in such circumstances. And it is human nature that the inmate will chip in with his own stories. Allan was careful and taciturn in speech but, as the conversation continued, he became more and more relaxed. He listened to me briefly then interrupted with accounts of his experiences in Southern Africa and all about how his first wife was shot in Zambia. He omitted to mention that he had shot her. Allan chatted about Egypt. He left out little details like poisoning his girlfriend there. He was a plausible and convincing liar.

I asked him if he was upset about the, 'tragic accident,' when his girlfriend died. 'Of course, I'm upset,' he commented indifferently. He gave a cynical grin and the most unconvincing shrug I ever saw in my prison career. 'It was nothing to do with me Mate,' he replied. 'They are saying it was murder. It was just an accident.' Again, he shrugged indifferently. 'Anyway, I've met another girl,' he boasted. 'She is really pretty and has got loads of money.' He gave a knowing wink. 'Another one I met her at the golf club,' he boasted with another unpleasant smirk.

I found it interesting that the most important matters in this case, as far as he was concerned, was the fact that he already had a pretty, new girlfriend. It was also interesting that one of the first things he mentioned about her was the fact that she had got, 'loads of money.' Apparently by then he was courting this second lady who, totally by chance, was also suffering from cyanide poisoning. What a coincidence! This is another classic behaviour pattern with psychopaths. They do not learn from experience. You would expect a man who had just committed a murder to behave himself. Our American colleagues have a very expressive, criminal, slang term to describe this.

'Keep your head down and lay low until the heat cools off.'

Far from laying low Allan was consorting with prostitutes and was in the process of poisoning his new girlfriend. As the chat continued Allan was obviously loosening up and he boasted that he had been involved in gun running and had been a mercenary. He also explained that he had worked for British Intelligence in Africa. There is another condition in psychopaths in which they relate stories which they would like to be true. This is wish fulfilment and it is known as Pseudologia Fantastica. The golden rule of telling lies is that the liar must know more about the subject that he is telling lies about than the person who he is telling lies to. Allan could talk about Africa, but he knew little about guns or gun running. Or about being a mercenary. I have been a shooting man for most of my life and I once wrote a book about mercenaries. ('Do You Want to Live Forever?' published by Amazon.) Often such psychopaths will personalise stories when they steal some interesting or exciting anecdote from a book or film and recount it with themselves as the hero. I got the distinct impression that this was exactly what Allan was doing. When you listen to someone who is telling you some far-fetched yarn it is the job of an R.M.N. to judge, among other matters, whether they are telling the truth or not. You make this judgement on two totally different levels. The first is simple question, answer, and your own knowledge of the issue. A nineteen years old boy once told me that he was an ex-SAS man. He was lying. He was not old enough. The second level on which you judge a man is gut feeling. When you work in a job like mine on a regular basis it is impossible not to develop an instinct for when people are telling lies. Often, I have listened to a person telling some outrageous, far-fetched story and instinctively you know he is lying. Another man might tell you an equally far-fetched tale but nevertheless you still believe it. And later it turns out to be true. And just to complicate matters many people tell stories which have a basis in fact but are grossly exaggerated in detail. And to further complicate the issue many inmates are habitual and convincing liars who have spent a lifetime telling lies on every issue imaginable.

Quite casually Allan related how his girlfriend had died in Egypt and her body had been embalmed and then shipped home. He gave a rueful grimace. 'I didn't expect that,' he confessed sadly. I looked at him and, just for one moment there was a flash of genuine emotion in his face. I realised that he was not in the slightest bit concerned about his dead lady friend. He was worried about the autopsy findings. As a matter of fact, the embalming made the autopsy much more difficult and inconclusive. But he did not know this.

Just like lots of other psychopaths he had an advanced case of grandiosity. Allan asked me if I had been to university. Nowadays my qualifications would be

classed as University Degrees but when I passed my exams, they were simply

Nursing Qualifications. When I explained this, he eagerly interrupted me to

explain that he had trained and passed a degree in chemistry. He seemed to

think that this made him superior to me. Mind you Allan thought he was

superior to everyone. I would point out though, that I don't poison people. His

education in chemistry seems to have been a waste of public money except for

his expertise with and access to cyanide which helped him greatly when he

started murdering his lady friends.

I always believed that cyanide was a quick, painless end. When you read spy stories the Secret Agent always has his cyanide pill to ensure a quick death

when captured. As one would expect this is the usual rubbish that fiction writers

seem to specialise in. Apparently this poor girl died in agony. Allan simply

shrugged indifferently as he gave me his account of what he claimed had

happened. Apparently, he was with her when she died but, as one would expect,

his account differed radically from the newspaper reports. 'I did everything I

could to help her,' he protested.

Like many psychopaths, and like many ordinary people, his account was

heavily biased in his own favour. But he was adamant that he was innocent.

By the end of this interview I had come to some very firm conclusions.

I did not believe that he was mentally ill in any way. I did not refer him to a

psychiatrist.

In plain English he was a psychopath.

'How do you know he was not mentally ill?'

is the obvious question.

The answer to this question is both self-

evident and very interesting.

If a person is mentally ill, then they must have delusions and/or hallucinations

as well as thought disorder. A person with delusions is gripped with a need to

talk about them. If you really believe that Aliens from Outer Space or the

Russian Secret Service are chasing you, then it is almost impossible for a patient

with such strongly held beliefs to conceal them. Again, if you know that you

really are Jesus Christ then you tell everyone of the fact. Allan made no effort at

all to discuss any weird, wonderful or obviously false beliefs. He was oriented

for time and place. He did not show any thought disorder or muddled thinking.

His speech was calm and rational. There was no suggestion of any brain damage

or other organic impairment. He knew exactly where he was, what he was

charged with and why. His eye contact, facial expression, body language

and posture were all appropriate. I did not know the details of his case. I did know he was in serious trouble. But he assured me that he would, 'get a not

guilty.' It was obvious that he was taking clear, logical steps to avoid

conviction. He showed no regret or remorse whatever. Rarely, very rarely, a

person has a systematised delusional state in which a cleverly worked out false

belief is rationalised within a framework of reality.

The infamous killer, Peter Sutcliffe for instance believed that he had a God

ordained duty to kill prostitutes. But he also knew that he was living in England

in the 1970's and that the police would arrest him for murder.

So, he took great practical lengths to avoid capture. Interestingly, as his crimes

progressed, and his mental condition deteriorated, his behaviour deteriorated, and he began killing any unfortunate woman who crossed his path. Many of

these ladies were not even prostitutes. Not that it would have been any reason to

kill the poor girls even if they were.

I met this condition of a Systematised Delusional State just twice in my entire

career.

It is that rare.

John Allan had the same kind of unpleasant mood, manner and conceit that

Sutcliffe had. But he did not even have the excuse of mental illness. Allan was

hoping and expecting a not guilty result. For the reasons which I have already

described it is far more difficult than most people imagine to successfully pretend that you have a mental illness when you do not have one. But Allan did

not even claim to be mentally ill.

Many people believe whatever it is that they want to believe. This is called the

Cognitive Dissonance. Allan believed that he would get found not guilty. Mind

you he also took practical measures to try and avoid the penalties of his crime.

He was the proud possessor of a striking, full head of black hair and beard. One

day he visited the Jail barber and had the entire lot shaved off!

He was highly indignant when he was promptly escorted to be photographed

again. He protested vigorously at this, but the guards were adamant. It is a standard procedure that if any Cat 'A' inmate changes his outward appearance

in any way then he must immediately be re-photographed. Allan did not know

this. We received a phone call in the Healthcare Unit that, 'someone,' had told

an officer that Allan planned on having a heart attack that afternoon. He then

intended to escape from the outside hospital. He would have been far better off

in telling no-one and leaving his haircut and shave until he had escaped. Inmates

often come up with what they think is a new idea. It may well be a brilliant idea.

They forget that the Prison Service has been dealing with brand-new, brilliant

ideas for hundreds of years. Nevertheless, he obviously decided to go ahead

with his plan. By the time Allan reported sick and declared that he was having a heart attack and needed to be transferred to an outside hospital we were all

waiting for him.

To be fair he did try and look as if he was in pain.

He might have been a good chemist.

He was a lousy actor.

The golden rule of telling lies kicked in. He might have a degree in chemistry, but he knew nothing about medicine. The doctor took his blood pressure and pulse and informed him that these were completely normal.

The doctor then kindly gave him the good news that he was not having any kind of heart attack and could stay in Altcourse Prison. For some strange reason he seemed disappointed.

I can't imagine why.

By and large a huge waste of effort.

John Allan had no excuse whatever for his actions. He chose to commit

murder. He was responsible for what he did.

He is exactly where he belongs.

In jail!

Allan had the arrogant, unpleasant attitude that aggressive psychopaths carry around with them.

Was he guilty?

Yes! As guilty as hell!

Did he know what he was doing?

Certainly.

Did he know that it was illegal, immoral and evil?

Yes! Beyond a shadow of a doubt.

Did he deserve life imprisonment?

Beyond a shadow of a doubt.

When he got life imprisonment, he was very angry. He told me that he intended to appeal.

I told him that this was his privilege.

I don't know if he ever did bother appealing.

I do know that he remains exactly where he belongs.

In jail.

If you have ever been emotionally attached to a psychopath.

Ask yourself one simple question.

'With friends like this who needs enemies?'

SOME NEWSPAPER REPORTS ABOUT JOHN ALLAN

Tuesday 7th March 2000. Life for 'Death on the Nile' killer.

A lawyer named Lesley Lewis who dies in agony. An industrial chemist who

poisoned his wealthy lawyer girlfriend on holiday in Egypt has been jailed for

life. John Fredrick Allan, 48, had denied murdering his partner Cheryl Lewis at

the luxury New Winter Palace Hotel in Luxor. But he was found guilty by a

majority verdict at Liverpool Crown Court. Passing a life sentence, the judge,

Mrs Justice Smith, told Allan that she would recommend he serve 'a very long sentence.'

"This was a cruel and pre-meditated killing," she said.

In the privacy of your hotel room you abused the confidence and trust which

Cheryl Lewis placed in you as a partner and, in my view, you tricked her into

taking cyanide.

You must then have watched her suffer until she was beyond making a

complaint. The court heard Allan, from Wirral tricked her into taking cyanide in

a bid to inherit her £400, 000 fortune.

By RUSSELL JENKINS

John Allan was jailed for life yesterday for murdering his solicitor girlfriend with cyanide in their holiday hotel in Luxor, Egypt, after forging her will to

inherit her £460,000 fortune.

At the end of what became known as the "Death on the Nile" murder trial,

Allan, a 48-year-old industrial chemist, was told by the judge that the murder of

Cheryl Lewis (43) was "cruel and premeditated".

Allan slipped the cyanide into a nightcap gin and tonic and handed it to Miss

Lewis as she prepared for bed in room 508 of the Winter Palace Hotel in

October 1998, and then he watched her die in agony.

Mrs Justice Smith, at Liverpool Crown Court, said Allan must stay in prison for

'a very long time.'

Allan merely closed his eyes briefly as the jury delivered its verdict amid emotional scenes after 17 hours deliberation on the 35th day of the trial.

Merseyside Police were jubilant last night that they had ended the career of a

potential serial killer who used poison to reinforce his female victims'

dependence upon him.

Allan had disposed of Miss Lewis, a respected figure on Merseyside who ran

her own solicitor's practice, because she was looking to end their seven-year

relationship.

The court heard that Allan, who was financially dependent on Miss Lewis and

shared her home in Oxton, Birkenhead, north-west England, had been planning

the murder for 13 months, since August 1997, when he altered her will to make

himself the residual beneficiary.

Allan had worked in the mining industry in Africa where he would have gained

extensive knowledge of cyanide. Miss Lewis would have been in agony for

some minutes before lapsing into a coma-like state.

Allan, pretending to be distress, went to the hotel reception desk to tell staff

that his "wife" was dying.

THE GANGSTER.

Sean Jackman boasted to me that he

'owned,' a pretty, little, coastal town. This

was Southport. He bragged that he ran all

the drugs and rackets there. Exactly what

'rackets,' were prevalent in a law-abiding,

little place like Southport was never

established. He told me that the local police were all scared of him and he was paying them off. Many criminals boast that they are bribing police. Some of them are. Some of them are telling lies. It is interesting that this man described himself as the, 'gang leader,' who 'owned and ran,' Southport. That is obviously how he thought of himself and is also what he thought other people thought. In real life, of course, this is Fantasy Island rubbish. 'Big Gang Leaders,' do not work as nightclub bouncers. Nor do they commit murder. Real 'Big Gangsters,' own Security Firms who employ nightclub bouncers and they have minions who they pay to commit murder. Jackman was no gang leader. He was just an unpleasant, muscle-bound thug with an over-inflated sense of his own importance. Many inadequate people like this tell lies. The reason why is obvious and simple. They tell lies which they wish were true to bolster their own inadequate personalities. This is known as pseudologia fantastica. Jackman was over six feet tall, broad-built, weighed about twenty stone and had an aura of violence about him that frightened people. He told me that he was an expert in violence. He was! Two men annoyed him, so he battered one of them to death with a baseball bat. The bat broke over his victim's head and was unusable, so he killed the second man by smashing his head in with a metal fire extinguisher. The two victims had such appalling injuries as are normally found in road traffic accidents. There was even blood on the ceiling. And, for good measure, somebody had urinated on the bodies. Investigations led to this well-known criminal. A senior policeman commented. 'We had no motive for a couple of days. But as the investigation got going, we spoke to people who had seen the victims out drinking the previous night.' It was believed that the two deceased men had been 'acting inappropriately,' towards a girlfriend of one gangster who called his mate for help. These crooks used the same gym and worked together as bouncers. Both told different stories, and both blamed another man.

Referring to this case a Senior Police Officer stated. 'We have never known the exact sequence of events in that flat that day or who dealt what blows. The only people who know that are the people who were there.'

I should also mention one other small difference between this man and other inmates whom I met inside Her Majesty's Prison establishments. In the case of this man, unlike many other criminals whom I have met, No! I most certainly did not enjoy his company. Nor did I feel any empathy or sympathy for him. He

was just an arrogant, unpleasant, homicidal maniac. An evil, psychopathic killer

who believed he had a God given right to murder and mutilate anyone? When

you meet professional criminals of this type, one fact and one fact instantly,

comes to mind. You are glad that jail exists! Because that is where such people

belong. The general public, are consciously and subconsciously, brainwashed

by the media and badly written novels in which lovely, golden-hearted criminals

are portrayed as Robin Hood types who never harm anyone and who only steal

from 'the rich.' I have even heard the Kray Brothers being described in this

way. In real life such people are the worst type of criminal scum imaginable.

Jackman was arrested and while on remand he devised an ingenious plan to foil

justice. One of the chief prosecutions witness' against him was a young lady. It

was alleged that he had boasted of the killing to her. Apparently, she was going

to be subpoenaed and compelled to give evidence. But the gangster told me

emphatically that he had, 'taken care,' of this eventuality. At the time I

wondered if he was arranging to have her murdered. I submitted an S.I.R. form

concerning this possibility. (S.I.R. Security Intelligence Report; in jail any

member of staff can submit a report at any time about any matter which they

consider to be of security interest.) The gangster assured me that he would get a

'not guilty,' verdict. Under British law a woman cannot be forced to give evidence against her husband. So, he decided to marry her. When informed of

the planned marriage the Crown Prosecution Service immediately issued an

objection to the superintendent of registrars. But it is only possible to stop a

marriage on very clear grounds. If one partner is already married for instance, is

of unsound mind or is less than sixteen years of age. The Prison Service could

not stop the marriage because of this man's Human Rights. The CPS made legal

objections, saying it was against the public interest. The hearing took place in

secret and initially the marriage was banned. His lawyers took the case to

the Court of Appeal which found in his favour. The couple married in Altcourse

Prison the day before the trial started. The trial judge ruled that the woman could not be referred to in front of the jury. The Judge also ordered that the

media could not publish anything about this marriage.

A Police Superintendent stated. 'It could have been very damaging to the case. I

would like to see a review of the rules of evidence in respect of the non-

compellability of spouses."

I couldn't have put it better myself.

People criticise judges, but a judge can only enforce the law as it stands. They

cannot invent new laws as they go along. However, much they would like to.

Police and prison staff are in the same position. I once met a man in my local

Pub who shouted and swore at me because the Prison Service had released 'a

dangerous man,' who then committed another murder. The media was full of criticism of the Prison Service as this drunk informed me. Are these people mad

or just plain stupid? An e-mail or fax arrives from the Home Office ordering a

person's release and the officials of the Prison Service have no choice whatever

in the matter. When a prisoner has served his sentence, he MUST be released.

Any prison manager who refused to do so would be committing a criminal

offence himself.

This 'Big Gangster,' was brought to trial and he told me emphatically and

laughingly that he would, 'get the right verdict.'

Well I am happy to say that he most certainly did.

'How do you think you will get on in court?' I asked him on the day before the

verdict. I was genuinely curious.

'I'll get not guilty,' he boasted with a big grin. 'I'm paying off the judge,' he

lied, 'and I've got the jury in my pocket as well.'

It was patently obvious that he was telling lies. A big-time, professional

criminal bribing a judge or jurist would never go around telling people.

Fortunately, though even without his so-called 'wife's' evidence the case was

still strong enough to secure a conviction.

Jackman was cordially disliked by prison staff and on the day of his sentencing

I was on duty in the Admissions Unit when an officer gestured to a radio which

was giving an account of the case.

I listened with great interest and I could not help but grin as I listened to the

result.

Later that day he returned from court and came into my office. 'How did you get on?' I asked with an innocent face. Of course, I already knew.

He looked at me with a deadpan face. 'I got life imprisonment with a recommended minimum of twenty-five years,' he stated flatly.

Most people do not understand the difference between a sentence of imprisonment and a recommended minimum. If a man is sentenced to ten years in jail then he serves five. In this case a minimum of twenty-five years means he must serve that. He was thirty-three at the time. So! He would be fifty-eight before he could even apply for parole. And there is absolutely no guarantee that he will get it. I was tempted to say. 'Well if I were you, I'd ask the judge for my money back. Anyway, just relax. And I hope you enjoy your honeymoon?'

I didn't say any of this.

This man had been hoping and expecting a not guilty verdict. Many people

believe whatever it is that they want to believe. People also like to believe that

what they hope will happen WILL happen. This is basic human nature. It is

called the Cognitive Dissonance. But when someone gets a result like this then

the reaction varies tremendously. When a man receives such a sentence it takes

a day or so for the situation to really sink in. The shock is so intense that

initially you do not feel anything. It is like being punched by Mike Tyson. You

don't feel pain. You just feel numb. Then as the bad news sinks in then his reaction is more profound and intense. Reality rears its' ugly head. He might

become suicidal, violent, depressed, turn to religion, withdraw within himself.

Perhaps sit there sobbing and weeping. I have seen a man who just got a life

sentence curl up into the foetal position and start crying. I wondered exactly

what reaction the big gangster would display. I should have known. When

people are under severe stress they invariably exhibit an exacerbated trait of

whatever personality conditions are the most dominating in their lives. It could

be alcohol, drugs, religion, self-pity, aggression or any factor. I knew a man

whose wife died tragically, and he went through a period of having sex with any

and every available female. Obviously, he liked women, so he coped with his misery by having sex with absolutely any available female. I worked with

another nurse who lost her husband and for one year she worked continuous

twelve-hour shifts. In her case she buried herself in work. She kept herself

occupied and also made an awful lot of money.

In Jackman's life, of course violence ruled his entire life, personality and

behaviour. So! He became violent.

TWO DAYS LATER.

A First Response sounded from his Wing. (XX. FIRST RESPONSE; the First

Response is a red button sited on top of a staff radio. Every staff member who

has prisoner contact has a red button situated on top of their radio. If pressed for three seconds an emergency alarm cuts through all other radio traffic and the

Control Officer will shout, 'First Response,' along with the location. It is

reserved for an urgent appeal for help. My own call sign was usually Hotel

Seven and staff must check in with Control any change of location. That day it

Sounded, 'First Response. Reynoldstown Brown.' The First Response is a team

of three specially trained officers who will answer and sort the problem out. In

addition, any other spare staff usually respond.

The Admissions Unit was quiet when the alarm sounded. On occasion a First

Response may well be a false alarm but with experience it is easy to

differentiate. A cacophony of four-letter words accompanied by shouts, screams, swearing and threats is always a genuine alarm. 'Would you like to see

a First Response?' I asked a student. 'Just out of curiosity?'

We went to pay a visit. Sure, enough this charming man had totally lost control

of himself and was busily engaged in smashing up his own cell.

Who cares?

It was his cell.

He was being 'twisted up,' (restrained) by half a dozen, big, strong, prison

officers.

The officer holding his right arm must have weighed about thirteen or fourteen

stone and as I watched I saw this officer rise into mid-air. Jackman was lifting

him with one arm. In novels and movies, the hero, always wins his fights. Real life situations are far simpler. Another very large prison officer jumped onto his

arm as well. In situations like this the inmate never wins despite the puerile and

stupid propaganda put out by the media.

I personally, as well as most other prison and police staff, get very annoyed

when criminals such as this are portrayed as glamorous, folk heroes. And police

and prison staff are repeatedly described as corrupt, cowardly bullies.

Even idiots such as the man who calls himself Charles Bronson has been

portrayed as a charismatic rebel figure. Really, he is just a sad, pathetic,

inadequate loner who cannot cope outside of prison.

SEGREGATION.

I watched the big, tough, 'Hard Case,' who had boasted that he 'owned'

that pretty, little coastal town, as he was physically lifted off his feet and

dragged to the Segregation Unit.

When he got there, he was shoved, pushed, dragged and carried to a strip cell

where he burst into tears and sobbed his poor little heart out.

Did I feel sorry for him?

No! I did not.

Every single unpleasant thing that happened to this man was his own fault and

his own choice. He made a conscious decision to murder people. And he was a

professional criminal anyway. He enjoyed being, 'the Big Man' who everyone

knew and feared. (or so he thought) He loved playing the Movie Gangster.

Well! Chickens come home to roost. In a case like this the man is invariably

sent to a very High Security Jail where his fellow prisoners are just as violent

and as psychopathic as himself. Suddenly, sometimes for the first time in his

life, he is no longer, 'the Big Man.' Even a twenty-five-year stretch is nothing

special in such a place. Such prisoners cause big trouble at first, but they

always eventually settle down. No matter how long it takes.

Many so-called, 'big crooks,' boast and brag about how easy it is in jail

nowadays. They will show you a beautifully furnished, little cell which has a

large, colour television with numerous channels. They will show you their

collections of books and DVDs and boast about how they have access to illegal liquor, illicit pills and drugs. They will tell you all about the fantastic lives they

have led and boast of the elegant, glamorous, James Bond lifestyle. They will

tell you all about how much money they have got stashed away in Swiss and

Lichtenstein bank accounts.

What they will not tell you of is a sex life of nothing but masturbation, a social

life of once weekly visits from their loved ones and the constant and never-

ending waste of your life when you cannot even go for a walk without

permission. And perhaps ten, or twenty or maybe thirty years, later when the

man has spent endless, long, lonely nights staring at prison walls and thinking to

himself then he might realise the simple truth that many older crooks tell the young punks who idolise, and hero worship them.

I have heard it said a thousand times by old lags in their forties, fifties or

older and who now regret how they have wasted their lives.

'The cop only has to be EITHER smart or lucky JUST ONCE. The crook must

be BOTH smart AND lucky every single time.'

I didn't say any of this. All that would have done would be to make him angrier

and then some unfortunate prison officer or perhaps an innocent fellow prisoner

would be the object of his rage. But what was I supposed to do? Feel sorry for

him? Sit down and cry with him? Make unrealistic promises?

This man made a conscious choice to totally ignore the laws and morals of

society. Well! Welcome to the real-world. Society has decided to fight back.

What a complete and utter waste! Not just of his own life! But, much more

importantly, the lives of the two men he murdered. Not to mention the many

other innocent people who suffered because of his criminal actions.

I didn't say any of this. Instead I looked at my watch. It was nearly dinner time.

I walked over to the canteen, ordered a cup of tea, sat down, and ate a good

meal.

And if you asked me what I thought of it all?'

My answer would have been. 'Well! As prisons go the food in Altcourse is pretty good.'

I think I know how Pontious Pilate felt when he washed his hands.

THE FOOL.

Sometimes when working in a High-Security Jail there comes through, a lad or

man, who forever afterwards sticks in your mind.

This boy walked nervously into my office. 'Can I come in please Sir?' he asked

politely.

'Take a seat,' I invited him wearily. 'What are you in jail for?'

I knew it had to be serious. The paperwork told me that he was cat 'A' and he

was dressed in escape clothing. This is prison clothing with orange stripes down the arms and legs. He is wearing this because he escaped or attempted to escape.

This makes him easier to identify if he succeeds in getting away. He looked just

like the sort of naïve, frightened, young lad who, every so often, ends up in Her

Majesty's Prisons. He was tall, thin, good-looking, courteous well-spoken and

scared stiff. None of this is unusual.

'Well it's like this you see Sir,' the lad explained. 'It's all a big mistake. You

see I went on holiday.'

I gave an inward groan, 'Where to?' I asked.

'Well my friend and I worked together all summer,' he explained.

'Neither of us had ever been abroad before. We had just finished at college and

both wanted to somewhere special, so we saved up. The travel agents were advertising cheap holidays in a place called Columbia. In the brochures it

looked lovely.'

I shook my head in disbelief. 'Columbia,' I thought, 'of all places.'

'Then what happened?' I asked.

'Well the hotel was a bit of a dump Sir,' he explained. 'But there were lots of

other English people there and the alcohol was cheap. On my first night there I

was just sitting in the bar with my friend when this woman just started chatting

to me. She spoke good English and she had this lovely accent. I thought that she

was a lot older than me, but she told me that she was only twenty-four and she

said that Latin women look older because they are dark. She had a lovely figure

with big breasts, and she was wearing this low-cut dress. You could see absolutely everything. And she seemed really interested in me. She asked me all

about myself. 'Had I ever been abroad before? Had I ever had a girlfriend

before? What I studied at College?' Normally I am a bit shy with girls, but she

made me relax. She bought me a few drinks then took me for a walk. I couldn't

believe it when she started kissing me and telling me how much she fancied me.

I was sharing a room with my friend, but she took me back to her room. That

night we ended up in bed together. I'd never had sex with a girl before. It was

amazing. She told me that normally she would never dream of sleeping with a

boy who she had just met but the moment she saw me she fancied me and

wanted to make love to me. It was unbelievable. She told me that she had made love to one boy before me but that was all a mistake and that she loved me. She

did things to me that I'd never even dreamt of. I thought I'd died and gone to

heaven. We had this fantastic holiday romance. I couldn't believe it when she

said that she wanted to keep in touch after I went home. She said she would

come to England to see me. I was mad about her. At the beginning of the week I

thought that she might be one of these foreign women who you hear about. You

know the girls who chase English lads so that they can marry them for a British

passport. But she never once asked me for money. In fact, she had loads of

money herself. Her father was a rich businessman. She treated me to loads of

nice meals. One day I mentioned that I would love to go out on a boat trip, but I didn't have enough money. She paid for us both to go on a day-long cruise

together. God knows what that must have cost her. She was at university

training to be a nurse. Her family lived in the town. They lived in this posh

villa. It had a swimming pool, a tennis court, everything. She kept on saying

that we would get married and spend the rest of our lives together.'

I had to ask a question. 'Why was she staying in a hotel if her family lived so

close?' I inquired politely.

The lad looked puzzled and thought hard for a moment. 'I don't know,' he

replied. 'It never occurred to me to ask. Anyway, what does it matter?'

I was tempted to state. 'The reason why she was staying in this hotel was to recruit fools like you to act as drug couriers,' but I felt as if he had already

suffered enough. And, just for good measure he had a lot more suffering ahead

of him.

'What happened to the friend you went on holiday with?' I asked curiously.

'He was really angry with me,' the lad explained indignantly. 'Just because I

had met a beautiful girl, he was angry. He was like a big, soft kid. He did not

like her at all. But it was just jealousy. And my girlfriend did not like him

anyway. We had a big argument and he stormed off. We never spoke again.'

'What happened next?' I asked with genuine curiosity.

'At the end of the holiday she asked me to do her a favour. She wanted me to take a parcel back home to England with me. My girlfriend told me that lots of

people do this and none of them ever get caught. She said that even if I was

caught it was nothing serious. I would just get a fine. And she said she could

get me a thousand pounds for doing this little favour. She said it was just a way

for me to pay her back for all she had done for me. I knew I shouldn't really do

it, but she said that it was not that important,' the lad looked straight at me and

his eyes filled up with tears as he started crying. 'I thought we were in love,' he

confessed. The boy was openly weeping now. 'But I think that she was just

using me to smuggle drugs,' he admitted.

I gave the lad a couple of paper towels and he wiped his face and eyes. Then he looked straight at me again. 'I think I've been really stupid,' he confessed

slowly.

'A flash of intelligence,' I thought to myself.

I didn't say this.

'I was in love,' the boy protested quickly.

I gave another silent, inward groan. I had a mental picture of this beautiful,

sexy, middle-aged, Latin hooker with big breasts who was paid a lot of money

to seduce naïve, young English lads and at the end of the holiday ask them, 'to

do her a favour.'

'What happened next?' I asked suspiciously and wearily.

'Well I agreed to do this for her,' he explained. 'I got off the aeroplane. And as I

was walking through the concourse, I heard this dog barking. It ran straight up to me and then just sat there wagging its' tail. I could not understand what was

happening. Then all these men and women in uniforms came running towards

me.'

'What did you do?' I asked curiously. 'Did you run like hell?'

'No Sir,' he replied. 'I was puzzled. I wondered what on earth was going on.'

'Then what?' I asked.

'They searched me,' the Fool explained eagerly. His face fell. 'And they found

the parcel my girlfriend had given me.'

'Where did you have it hidden?' I asked.

I was expecting some intricate, deep, thought out, clever plan of concealment.

'In my pocket,' the lad explained eagerly, but as he admitted this his face fell again. He had a very expressive face. Many inmates, in jail both young and old

can lie convincingly but not this lad. I realised that he would have been a

pushover when faced with an experienced hooker or for that matter with

customs and police in England. Mind you in one way he was very lucky. If he

had been arrested in Columbia, he would have found that British jails are

heaven compared with South American ones.

'What was in the package?' I asked. I had already guessed. 'Columbia of all

places,' I thought again.

'It was a bright, white powder,' he continued, 'and they arrested me. I was

charged with drug smuggling.' They called the police and I told the police officer all about my girlfriend. She had promised that someone would meet me

off the plane to collect this package but when the police tried to find him in

Arrivals he never turned up.'

The boy obviously did not know, or realise, that in a case like this the gang will

have another passenger on the same flight whose job it is to follow the smuggler

through customs. He will be unknown to the stooge and his job is simply as

observer. He himself will be clean. If the Fool gets through undetected then the

gang will contact him and ask for their package. Sometimes they will even pay

him so that they can use him again. But if he is caught then the watcher

immediately phones his colleague waiting for the plane as well as his friends back home. By the time the ponderous machinery of Interpol and the

Columbian Police have swung into action the 'friend' waiting to meet the flight

and his 'girlfriend' not to mention her 'mother and father,' are all long gone.

'I was really frightened when they took me to the police station,' the lad

continued tearfully. 'But the police there were really nice to me. One of them

told me that the best thing I could do was to tell the absolute truth, so I did.' The

boy started crying again. 'They put me in jail for the night and the next day I

appeared before the magistrate. I was hoping to get a caution. One of my friends

got a caution once for smoking cannabis. But instead they remanded me and

sent me to a Borstal. (In fact, the term Borstal has now been replaced with the term, 'Young Prisoner's Institution,' but most people, both staff and inmates

still use the old term.) 'One of the boys was alright with me,' he explained. 'But

the rest of them were making fun of me because they said I, 'talked posh.' And

some of them were horrible to me. One of them threatened to knife me just

because he said he didn't like the way I looked at him. Some of the other lads

were saying that I would get raped. And they said that the screws would never

interfere because they are all taking bribes off the inmates to turn a blind eye.'

Again, I gave a silent inward groan. This kind of so-called joking is common in

such places. It is always described by the participants as 'harmless fun.' It is not

in the least bit of harmless fun for the helpless and hapless fool who believes every word. People like this silly little boy who had obviously swallowed the

whole yarn; hook, line and sinker. He obviously believed not only the

Columbian hooker but also these idiots. The lad paused and then resumed his

sobbing. 'So, I escaped from the Borstal,' he continued. 'It was really easy. All

I had to do was to wriggle under the wire at the back of the place. Apparently, it

was an open prison. But! I'm afraid I was not out for very long.'

'How long?' I asked gently.

'Well I started hitch hiking,' he went on. 'A couple of cars went by but then

another one stopped for me. I couldn't believe my luck. But the driver did a U-

turn and took me straight back to the Borstal. The driver was a prison officer

going home for his dinner.'

I had to ask. 'Where would you have gone to if you had got away?'

The lad thought for a moment. 'Well I would have gone to my parent's house,'

he replied. He was so naive and innocent he obviously did not realise that this

was the first place the police would look.

So, they locked me up in the punishment block,' the Fool continued. 'And the

next day the forensic report on the drug came back. It was over ninety percent,

pure,' the lad hesitated. 'I don't quite know what that means,' he confessed.

(This means that ninety percent of the powder was pure cocaine as opposed to

street rubbish which is mostly sugar, salt, brick dust or any other muck. This is

an incredibly high purity content. Nowadays with modern drug testing methods a drug can be instantly identified but this all happened some time ago when

suspect substances still had to be sent off for analysis.) The lad paused to choke

back some more sobs. 'Then the police interviewed me again,' he explained.

'And apparently the address where my girlfriend and her parents' lived was a

rented villa. None of the neighbours had ever met them or even heard of them.'

The boy paused again. 'So now I am a category 'A' prisoner because the street

value of the drug was over a quarter of million pounds sterling,' he explained

slowly. 'And because I ran away from jail I am also on the 'escape list.' He

looked at me. 'Whatever all that means,' he protested slowly.

For a moment while listening to this tale I debated with myself if the Fool had been used simply as a red herring. Sometimes a drug gang will set up such an

idiot who is designated to be caught. He is the patsy and some gangsters

calculate that the customs will then relax, and the real smuggler will pass

through undetected. But of course, a fall guy like this will only be carrying

small amounts of poor-quality narcotics. Not a large amount of pure. And,

in real life customs people never relax. Customs personnel are far smarter than

that. And most modern crooks are far smarter than that. That is why stupid fools

like this boy are the ones who take the rap while the big boys sit back and laugh.

'Have you seen a brief?' I asked.

'What is a brief Sir?'

'A solicitor.'

'Oh yes,' the boy gave another inane grin. 'He told me I will get ten or twelve

years in jail.' The lad started crying again. 'They can't do that to me. Can they,

Sir?'

'Yes, they can,' I promised grimly.

The boy paused in his story. 'Apparently I am in big trouble,' he confessed. He

looked straight at me and wiped away his tears. 'Do you think my girlfriend will

wait for me Sir?' he asked seriously.

It took me a moment or two to realise that, 'his girlfriend,' who he was referring

to, was the middle-aged hooker who had stitched him up for ten or twelve years

in jail. 'I have sent several letters to her Sir,' the lad explained. 'But so far I

have not had an answer.' I wondered vaguely what address he had sent the letters to. One thing was for sure. Wherever it was the 'girlfriend' would never

go near the place.

I decided to tell him the truth. I owed him that much. 'She was not, and never

would be, your girlfriend,' I explained as gently as I could. 'She is a prostitute

and you will never see her again ever. By now she will be in another hotel, in

another town in Columbia, with another name, screwing some other, stupid,

young, English lad and asking him to 'do her a favour, by taking a parcel

through customs.'

The boy sat and gaped at me in honest, open-mouthed horror.

There was one last job I had to complete before I finished with him. 'When you

had sex with this woman?' I inquired. 'Did you use condoms?'

The boy looked puzzled. 'No,' he told me, 'there was no point! She told me she would be alright,' the lad answered. Again, the Fool looked puzzled but then, suddenly, a flash of comprehension came over his face and he appeared to understand me. 'My God!' he ejaculated in a horrified tone of voice. 'Do you think she could be pregnant?"

For a moment I felt like bursting out laughing. But I felt as if the lad had suffered enough already. 'Don't worry about that,' I ordered. 'I am absolutely certain that she is not pregnant.'

The lad gave an obvious sigh of relief. Then he looked at me in surprise.

'What's the problem then?' he asked.

'I will make you an appointment to see our Nurse Practitioner in STDs for you to be tested for any venereal diseases.' I explained. (S.T.D. Sexually

Transmitted Diseases.) He stared straight at me in dawning comprehension and

I will never forget the look of horror which and genuine understanding which

suddenly flashed across this lad's face.

Did I feel sorry for him?

As a matter of fact, strange to say.

Yes. I did.

I never found out what happened to him.

THE LIAR.

Melling Wing was the Youth Custody wing of Altcourse Prison. There were

two separate sides to this Wing. The Brown Side held boys aged fifteen to eighteen and they were called Young Offenders. The Blue Side held boys aged

eighteen to twenty and they were called Young Prisoners. In the old days these

places were called Borstals and the prisoners were variously called the lads, the

inmates, the trainees and various other, usually unprintable terms. Inside, such

institutions the macho cult rules among the boys. There were constant situations

in which boys would offer to fight other boys. Usually this was done in a

supposedly 'joking' manner. This was so that the challenger could back down if

his victim reacted in the wrong way. In an all-boys school, the toughest lad in

the year is the 'cock of the year' in a young lad's jail it is 'the Daddy of the

Wing.'

A closed jail is a Total Institution. There are four main activities of daily living.

These are sleeping, eating, working and recreation. In Total Institutions this all

takes place in one establishment. It might be a jail, an army camp, a ship, an

abbey, a Public School. In a Borstal Institution the macho cult is even more

extreme simply because the inmates are younger and by simple definition more

violent and more brutal. Young lads can be horrible in the extreme. We all

remember our school days when some evil-tempered bully would make life

unbearable for others. And, of course in jail it is impossible to walk away from

such stress.

An open jail is a place where the inmates are allowed weekend to leave and day passes. This is not a Total Institution. These are some of the reasons why many

prisoners want to serve their stretch in the Hospital Wing. In Altcourse the

Hospital Unit held a maximum of fourteen inmates but often there were only

two or three inmates there. In all prisons the hospital wing is regarded as a

'cushy number.' There is no compulsory work. The facilities are regarded as

being better. The staff tend to be more easy-going. Also, unlike the Rule 43

Wing which is where Nonces are kept there is no disgrace in being admitted to

'the Hospital.' If you serve time on a VP Wing (VP Vulnerable Prisoners) such

as Reynoldstown Blue then you are, forever, known as a Nonce. This is quite

unfair as many such prisoners are in for ordinary crimes but are under threat for some other reason. I knew one Altcourse prisoner was a close relative of a

murder victim. He gave evidence at the trial and was responsible for several

killers being jailed. But he could not be placed on normal location because there

was a Hit Contract out on him and some of the men, he had given evidence

against were serving time in the same jail. Such men also have friends and

relatives who can be just as much of a threat. So, he had to go, 'on the

Numbers.' People who are being bullied are also placed on this wing along with

sex offenders who may have committed heinous crimes. So, you have an odd

situation where bullies are placed together with the bullied. For some strange

reason it seems to work.

One day a new lad came into my office in Admissions. Like many young boys

he was tearful and upset. 'I shouldn't be here. It's all a mistake. I need help!'

These are remarks I have heard literally thousands of times. A very kind-

hearted, but rather naive, female Nurse took him to one side and interviewed

him. I have always been able to listen to two conversations at once and while I

was talking to another man I also listened as this new lad told the lady his story.

'The last time I was here Miss, I hanged myself,' he complained tearfully.

I was tempted to sarcastically state. 'Well you didn't make a very good job of

it.' The female nurse obviously believed his hard luck story. She admitted him

to the Prison Hospital Unit.

In a quiet moment I asked her politely. 'Why have you admitted this boy to the Healthcare Wing?"

'I felt sorry for him,' she explained. 'He has been in custody before and, last time he was inside he was bullied on Melling Wing,' she gave a sad grimace.

'He needs help,' she explained sorrowfully.

As politely as I could I explained that the Hospital Wing is for inmates who are suffering from an ILLNESS, whether mental or physical. It is not for people who are sad, lonely or just unhappy!

'If you can't do the time? Don't do the crime.'

The next day I was on duty in the Hospital Unit when Bang-Up ended. In plain English, the inmates were unlocked. I made a point of talking to the boy in question. He had a grin on his face like the proverbial Cheshire cat and he was

laughing and joking and chatting freely about his criminal past. He boasted

about crimes he had committed and about 'his team,' who were all 'sound lads,'

who could all be relied on 'to keep their traps and shut,' and, if necessary 'to go

down the steps like a man.' He was no more mentally ill than I was. People are

always puzzled as to how anyone can assess mental illness so quickly, but the

reasons are clear and obvious.

The first reason is experience. I worked in the field of psychiatry for thirty-eight

years. Even if I was an appalling Mental Health Nurse, I must have learnt

something in all that time. The second reason is simple questions and answers.

Most prison inmates, particularly young lads, know absolutely nothing about

psychiatry. They usually get as far as, 'I hear voices.' Or many of them will

say,' I feel like I am two different people.' This is because nearly everyone in

the Western World has seen movies or read books about Jekyll and Hyde and

they think that this is how to mimic mental illness. When a Mental Health Nurse

sees a person acting just like a person on the movies who is supposed to be

insane then you can guarantee that the person if faking. An actor or actress on

film or television is not insane. He/she is doing what they are told to do by a

producer/director who wants to make a good movie? And, in all probability the

scriptwriter also knows absolutely nothing at all about mental illness either. All of this may produce a good movie, but the film is light years away from reality.

Some boys will say. 'I think that people are after me.' This statement is also an

immediate give away. A real paranoid patient never says this. Instead he will

always say. 'People ARE after me.' The genuinely mentally ill person KNOWS

that people are chasing him. He does not say 'I THINK,' people are after me.

He KNOWS that someone is after him.

But after making these statements the malingerer is stumped. I spoke to the lad

for about thirty minutes. He did not display hallucinations or delusions. He was

orientated for time and place. His speech was clear, lucid and logical. His body

language, posture, eye contact and facial expression gave no sign or symptom of any mental illness. In short there was absolutely nothing wrong with him. He

was not even bothering to put an act on. The reason why he was not putting an

act on was obvious. He did not realise that I was a Mental Health Nurse. He

thought I was a Prison Officer. Even in this modern day and age many people

still subconsciously believe that a 'nurse' is a woman. I often had the experience

in prisons of being mistaken for a Doctor or Prison Officer. A female doctor

who I worked with was constantly mistaken for a nurse.

DOCTOR NO.

When the prison doctor, also known as Dr No, came in I gave him the handover.

He was extremely puzzled as to why anyone would admit a boy 'because she felt sorry for him.' I explained, and he was angry. I don't blame him. So was I.

'Someone should speak to that woman and explain the situation to her,' he

stated grimly.

'I already have done,' I explained.

I repeated the conversations of the lad that morning and further described his

behaviour and attitudes. 'Bring him here,' the Doctor ordered.

I walked up to the young lad. He was playing pool in the dining room. As he did

this he was talking and laughing with two other inmates.

'The doctor is here,' I explained. 'He wants to see you.'

The lad followed me into the office and faced the doctor. He now appeared to

be. What a surprise! In a very dejected state. His shoulders were hunched, he was crying, his eye contact was non-existent, and he was sobbing and stating

that he was depressed, mentally ill and intended to kill himself.

Dr No told the lad that he had been assessed by a psychiatric nurse and was now

fit for normal location.

'But no! I aint' seen no nurse Boss,' the lad expostulated quickly. 'The only

nurse I've seen was the lady last night.'

I explained that I was a trained and experienced Mental Health Nurse and the

lad was very annoyed. Suddenly, his facial expression changed totally, and he

glared at me in sheer anger. 'I thought you were a screw,' he protested

indignantly.

'What difference would it make if you knew that I was a Mental Health Nurse?"

I inquired.

He glared at me in sheer hatred. All of us knew the answer. It was obvious.

But he could hardly say. 'Well if I had known that you were a Psychiatric Nurse

then I would have lied through my back teeth and told you all about how

depressed and suicidal I am. I would have told you all about how I am hearing

the voices. But you have spoilt that you bastard. I thought that you were a

Prison Officer. I thought that this was just an informal chat. So, I relaxed and

told the truth.'

The Doctor spoke to the lad quite civilly. Which was more than I felt like

doing?

'You have been fully assessed,' he explained. 'You are not mentally ill. You will be transferred to Melling Wing.'

'But when I spoke to the lady last night, she said that I would serve my sentence

on the hospital wing,' he protested tearfully.

'She did not promise you any such thing,' I interjected. 'She promised that you

would be admitted for observation. You have been observed and you are not

mentally ill. So, you are going to ordinary location.'

The boy glared at me in sheer hatred. 'A while back you were laughing and

joking and telling me all about your crimes and how you and your mates were

the 'Top Boys' in your town,' I pointed out. 'Then when you saw the Doctor

you suddenly burst into floods of tears. And now the reason why you are getting

really angry is because you are not getting what you want.'

The lad gave me another malevolent glare.

'Take him away and transfer him to Melling,' the doctor ordered.

Outside the office the boy turned to me. 'What happens if I refuse to go the

Melling?' he asked me nastily. I could but help but grin. He had totally

abandoned the, 'little boy lost,' look that he had adopted for Mary and the

Doctor.' Again, he glared at me.

'You are going to Melling,' I stated flatly. 'You don't have any choice in the

matter.'

'What if I refuse?" he persisted. 'You can't make me.'

'If you refuse,' I explained. 'Then I will call three prison officers over here and

one of them will ask you nicely to accompany them to Melling. If you still refuse, then you will be given a direct order. If you refuse to obey a direct order

then you will be jumped on, twisted up and dragged kicking and screaming to

Segregation Unit where you will be nicked and placed on a charge for refusing a

direct order. And Seg is far stricter than Melling.' I shrugged. 'Personally, I

couldn't care less,' I explained. 'I get paid whatever happens. So, make your

mind up.'

When the lad was told to pack his kit and get transferred, he simply obeyed

orders. He was on Melling before bang-up ended.

This behaviour was not just me being unpleasant and nasty although jail does

affect you like that. In the world in which we live it would be lovely if no one ever was sent to any kind of custody. But unfortunately, people are jailed. And

when they get there, they try every ploy in the book to get out of the

consequences of their actions. This boy was just one of many such.

Later that day I explained to Mary exactly what had happened.

'But he told me that he was ill,' she protested. 'He has problems. He said to me,

'I need help.'' She was both annoyed and upset.

'Yes, I know all that,' I replied.

'Well if he said all of that to you then you should have kept on the hospital

unit?' she protested.

'Why?' I asked.

'Because he has problems,' she protested.

'His problem is that he does not like being in jail,' I explained

'How can you say that? She asked indignantly. 'And how do you know

anyway?'

'Because he tells lies,' I explained gently. 'I am a Mental Health Nurse,' I

pointed out. 'And I am specifically trained and experienced to spot liars.'

'But I felt sorry for him,' she protested. 'I wanted to help him.'

'His problem was that he does not like being in jail,' I repeated. 'The help that

he wanted was to spend his entire stretch on the Hospital Wing. You can't give

that, and you should not have given him the impression that you could. Even

though you did not actually make that promise he believed that you had. He believed this because that was what he wanted to believe. I told you that this

would happen. He was just looking for a cushy number. You did not help him in

anyway whatever. All you did was to give him false hope.'

She was extremely annoyed with me.

Mind you. I was extremely annoyed with her.

THE SOLDIER.

The number of people who you meet in jail, and for that matter in society

generally, who claim to be ex-SAS men, or ex-MI5 men or something similar is

simply phenomenal. The interesting thing is that these people do not seem to

realise that, behind their backs, everyone is killing themselves with laughter at them. The other side of the coin is the person who you sometimes meet. This

new admission was not particularly tall or well-built, nor did he boast of all

sorts of legendary adventures in the Falklands, Northern Ireland or other wars.

He simply marched smartly into my office, snapped to attention with his thumbs

down the seams of his trousers, stood three paces in front of my desk, rapped

out his full name and prison number and called me, 'Sir.' I knew that he had to

be ex-armed forces. Instinctively and instantly I knew that this man was for real.

He had just been sentenced to five years for armed robbery. On the issue of his

sentencing he was extremely lucky. The judge took his previous good character

and excellent military service into account.

I found this man very interesting. After his admission I saw him lots of times.

We had numerous chats together. It was difficult to get him to talk freely but

when we did get chatting, he was a good conversationalist.

On one occasion we sat together at a dining room table and listened while an

Irish prisoner started rabbiting on about, 'the War in Northern Ireland.' An

appreciative audience gathered round to listen. In jail prisoners love a good

debate. Often there is very little else to do.

Several inmates expressed disgust at the tactics and methods used by the I.R.A.

and declared that since ample opportunities were open to the Republicans to use

legitimate forms of protest then there was no need for violence.

The Irishman disagreed with them all. 'The vast majority of people in both Northern and Southern Ireland support the IRA one hundred per cent,' he protested vigorously.

'If so many Catholic people in Ulster and Southern Ireland support the IRA as you say then why don't they stand for Parliament and get elected?' my soldier friend asked.

The Irishman did not answer this question. Instead he went off on a tangent.

'The Republican Army is totally justified in fighting this war,' he replied. 'In France and Belgium in the 1940's the resistance fighters there used the same tactics as the IRA uses in Northern Ireland. When there is a war on people get killed. We have no choice. It is the only possible way we can fight back against the British Army of occupation.'

'Well if there is a war on why you are complaining when British soldiers shoot

back?' the soldier asked mildly.

Again, as one would expect, the Irishman dodged this question.

'What about Bloody Sunday?' he answered angrily.

(BLOODY SUNDAY; an episode when British Paratroopers fired on an illegal

demonstration in Northern Ireland in 1972. Thirteen men were killed.

Afterwards the Irish Catholic community called this, 'deliberate, cold-blooded

murder.' The British Army contested that the men were armed and shooting at

the soldiers. It is still a hotly debated issue.)

'Those bloody murderers shot innocent people for no reason whatever,' the

Irishman snarled viciously. 'Bloody assassins! They fired indiscriminately into

a crowd of innocent women, children and old men.'

I was watching the face of the soldier as the Irishman gave us his version of

Irish history. 'How many people were in that mob?' the soldier asked quietly.

'Thousands and bloody thousands,' the Irishman shouted.

'The IRA claimed that the crowd consisted of over fifteen thousand people, 'the

soldier replied.

'That's right,' the Irishman shouted.

'Every single person shot dead that day was male and aged between seventeen

and forty-one?' the soldier stated truthfully. 'The British troops were using 7.62

calibre rifles which fire with a muzzle velocity of over three thousand-foot pounds and a bullet speed of over three thousand feet per second. And not one

single woman, child or old man died that day. Yet half of the crowd was female,

lots of them were children and there were plenty of old men. So, it cannot

possibly have been indiscriminate firing.'

The Irishman looked distinctly disgruntled at this comment and he thought for a

moment before replying. 'Those men were all unarmed. Not one single gun was

recovered from any of the dead men,' he pointed out truthfully.

'Well considering that the entire mob consisted of IRA supporters any gun

would have been quickly grabbed and handed back to the boyos,' the soldier

retorted. 'The last thing the Provisional's want is to lose guns. And anyway, it is far better propaganda for the I.R.A. if the men who were shot were unarmed.'

'Not one of the dead men had any gunshot residue on their hands,' the Irishman

claimed truthfully.

'Gunmen in Northern Ireland always wear gloves while shooting,' the soldier

explained patiently. 'Both to prevent fingerprints on guns and to hide any

forensic evidence such as gunpowder traces. And before a body or wounded

man was handed over to the hospital you can be sure his friends would have

removed incriminating material, such as gloves, masks, guns or ammunition.'

The Irishman looked and obviously was, very angry. 'Well what about those

murders in Gibraltar,' he shouted. 'When the bloody SAS assassinated three, unarmed, Irish civilians for no reason whatever.'

'They were neither unarmed nor where they civilians,' the soldier explained

patiently. 'They were members of the General Headquarters Staff of the

Provisional IRA. They were in possession of a hundred and forty pounds of

Semtex. That does not make them 'unarmed civilians,' nor is it 'no reason

whatever,' to shoot them!''

'The bloody British should never have shot them at all,' the Irishman shouted.

'They should have been arrested.'

The soldier regarded his adversary calmly. 'You just said that there is a war on,'

he pointed out. 'You just said that people get killed in wars.'

'But they surrendered,' shouted the Irishman indignantly. 'I saw an account on television when a witness described how an IRA man had his hands in the air

when a soldier shot him.'

'That witness was over a hundred metres away,' the soldier explained. 'The

speed of sound is much slower than the speed of light so what the woman saw

was the Irishman being shot which made him rebound backwards with his hands

being flung upright. The witness was genuinely under the impression that he

had held his hands up in surrender and then, a moment or so later she heard the

sound of the pistol bullets. So, it appeared that the soldier shot him after he had

put his hands up. In fact, he was shot before he did this,'

The Irishman skilfully dodged this issue as well. Instead he went off on another tangent. 'What about the 'shoot to kill policy in Northern Ireland,'' he snarled,

'hundreds of innocent people were murdered by the bloody SAS?'

'If there is a shoot to kill policy in Northern Ireland why are there dozens of

IRA men in British jails? According to you the British Army would have shot

them all?'

'Even the bloody British Government had to admit that there was a, 'shoot to

kill policy,' the Irishman shouted. 'Hundreds of innocent people murdered by

the SAS.'

'SIX men were shot during the, so-called, 'shoot to kill policy,' the soldier

pointed out. 'That is not, 'hundreds,' of people. And five of them were

acknowledged members of the Provisional IRA or the INLA.' (INLA the Irish

National Liberation Army. An extreme, and even more violent, splinter group

from the Provisionals.) 'And they were shot by the RUC not by the SAS.

Incidentally what about the shoot to kill policy of the IRA? When did they ever,

keep the laws of war?' The soldier faced the other man calmly. 'Is there a war

on or not?' he asked.

'Bloody right there is a war on,' was the answer.

The soldier gave another sigh. 'You don't arrest people in wars,' he pointed out.

'You kill them. If there is a war on, then why can't British soldiers shoot back at

the IRA men who are trying to shoot them?'

'Because the British government claim that Ulster is a civil situation,' the

Irishman shouted in reply. 'Look at the way that I am being treated in here,' he yelled indignantly. 'I should be treated as a prisoner of war under the Geneva Convention.'

The soldier glanced around at the audience. 'According to the IRA,' he explained. 'When the IRA shoot British soldiers there is a war on. But when armed British soldiers confront an armed IRA man, they should arrest him because there is NOT a war on. And then when he is arrested the IRA man wants to be treated as a prisoner of war, because there IS a war on.' The soldier glanced around the crowded table at the other inmates and then at me. 'They don't want much do they Boss?' he inquired politely.

The Irishman was highly indignant. He himself then turned to me. 'He can't insult me like that,' he complained. 'I am a member of the Irish Republican

Army. I am a prisoner of war.'

The soldier gave a grin. 'We all read the newspapers,' he explained to the

surrounding crowd. 'This man is nothing to do with the IRA. He is a drug addict

and he is in jail for housebreaking!'

The entire audience roared with laughter.

MONTHS LATER.

'Do you ever miss the army?' I asked the old soldier one day.

He smiled sadly. 'Every minute of every day of my life,' he confessed. 'I joined

the army when I was sixteen years old. It has been my entire life. It is all I

know. I was thirty-six years old when I took my discharge. I had big plans for civilian life but all I did was sit in the British Legion listening to a gang of old

age pensioners talking about the Second World War.' The man stared straight at

me. 'I was on the verge of becoming an alcoholic,' he admitted. 'I've nothing

against old codgers like that. But I'm still a young man. I need something more

in life. I was planning on re-enlisting when I got caught up in that stupid,

bloody robbery.'

'What are your plans when you get out?' I asked.

The man shrugged. 'It will be really difficult to get a job with a police record

like mine,' he admitted.

'Do you have any particular qualifications?' I asked curiously.

The soldier considered for a long minute. 'I got the top grade in my entire company in C.Q.C,' he stated quietly. (C.Q.C. shorthand for, 'Close Quarter Combat.' In other words, silent killing and fighting with your bare hands.) I gave a wry grimace at that.

'Any other skills?' I inquired.

He himself considered for another moment. 'I am a trained sniper,' he explained. 'And I have a certificate for interrogating prisoners of war.'

I thought for a moment, 'how old are you?' I asked.

'I'm nearly forty Boss,' he answered. 'And I'm due out in a couple of months. All I know is the military. It's been my entire life since I was a teenager.'

'Have you ever thought of joining the French Foreign Legion?' I suggested seriously.

The man stared straight at me. 'I'm too old,' he pointed out.

'You could be generous about your age,' I suggested. 'Just knock a few years

off. You look really fit and well. If you pass the medical and are fit enough,

then I am sure that they will take you.'

'Do you know Boss,' he stated thoughtfully, 'I might do that.'

SOME MONTHS LATER.

During another talk he told me. 'I've been thinking things over. I have a British

Army pension which is mounting up while I am in here. I am spending nothing

right now. If I joined the Legion and did ten years, then I would be over fifty. If

had a French army pension as well then at that age I could well afford to retire. I could join one of these dating agencies and find a woman. There are lots of

pretty girls out there looking for a man. I've had an interesting life. I would

soon find a girl who fancies me.'

The old soldier looked around at the grey stone walls and iron bars that

surrounded him and gave a wistful look. Just for a moment I could guess what

he was thinking about. I knew that he was reflecting on good times in far off

lands and the camaraderie and fellowship he had lost and left behind him.

'I find myself thinking a lot,' he confessed. 'In jail you have plenty of time to

think. I was born in a country town. I expect it has changed a lot since I last

visited but maybe when I retire, I could go back and buy a little cottage there.'

The soldier smiled. 'And maybe a farming job to keep me busy. I worked on the

land as a kid. It would be great to do that again. I might even be able to afford a

little smallholding.'

'It sounds a lot better than armed robberies,' I replied.

ONE YEAR LATER.

It was well over a year after this man had been discharged from Altcourse Jail

that a postcard arrived at the prison. It was sent from an obscure African

country. It was addressed to me at the Healthcare Unit and my name was mis-

spelled. It was concise and to the point. As one would expect from a trained

soldier!

'Took your suggestion Boss. Knocked ten years off my age and joined the

Foreign Legion. Feel as if I have come home. Thanks for the advice. See you in

nine years. Maybe we will have a pint together one day. Best of luck.'

I sometimes wonder what happened to the people whom I met in my career.

This man probably completed his ten years in the Legion, by which time he

would be over fifty. If he was still alive then he might well have returned to

England married a nice lady and settled down to farming.

I hope he is living happily in that little, country town. On the other hand, maybe

he got killed in some distant land, fighting a forgotten war, in a lost cause. The

type of war the French government always uses the Legion in.

Well! If that was the case? It was his choice.

At least he died happy.'

THE SAILOR.

When new men come into Prison, they bring with them the behaviour patterns

which they have learned in their previous lives. Sometimes these patterns are

totally useless in prison and indeed may be counterproductive as all they

achieve is to make the new lad unpopular with staff and inmates. The

whingeing, whining, mummy-spoilt, little, rich boy receives the very least

sympathy.

A new man walked briskly into my office, snapped to attention and stood

\smartly, three paces in front of the desk with his thumbs down the sides of his t rousers.

'Take a seat,' I requested.

'Thank you, Sir,' the man replied as he sat down.

He was big, broad, well-built and middle-aged with a large, black beard

and faded tattoos on both arms. One tattoo was of an old sailing ship. He

carried himself with the unconscious air of authority that shouted ex-N.C.O.

'Royal Navy?' I inquired.

The man grinned. 'Aye-aye Sir,' he acknowledged. 'Chief Petty Officer!

Twenty-four years. Do I call you Sir?' he inquired politely.

'Well you can call me Chris,' I explained. 'But if you are talking to a prison

officer and you don't know his or her name then just stick to Boss and Miss.

Avoid terms like mate and pal. If you get friendly with an officer and he says,

'call me Bill or Joe,' that is fine but if you don't know their name stick to Boss

and Miss and you can't go wrong.'

'Yes Boss,' he rapped out smartly.

It transpired that this man was on his first custodial sentence. He had received a

one year stretch that day. I explained that, since it was his first time and it was

not for an offence of violence, he could be out in four months if he behaved. He

was pleasantly surprised. I gave him the usual talk I always gave to new men

and he listened attentively, thanked me politely and went on his way.

ONE MONTH LATER.

Crossing the courtyards, I met this man again. I stopped to chat. 'How are you getting on?' I inquired.

The big man laughed. 'Everything is fine thanks Boss,' he replied. 'In fact, after

basic training in the Royal Navy twenty-five years ago this place is a piece of

cake.'

'Any problems?' I asked.

'Oh, a couple of weeks ago some little shit on the wing got funny with me Boss

so, I …' the man hesitated for one, long moment and then grinned.

'Yes?' I prompted. The sailor grinned again.

'I had a quiet word with him Boss,' he stated with a quick wink. He looked

closely at me. 'After all I'm only serving four months Boss,' the sailor

explained politely. 'Most of the screws here are decent people. Many of them are ex-forces just like me. I want to get out as soon as possible. I've got a wife

and three kids out there. Not to mention a business that I want to get back to.

My wife told the kids I am working away and fortunately my case was not

reported in the newspapers, so, I want to put all of this behind me and get back

to my life.' The old sailor paused. 'There are a couple of young punks on the

Wing who try and cause trouble for anyone and everyone,' he explained. 'And

one day some little shit started calling me a suck-hole and a creep just because I

am polite to staff.'

I wondered vaguely exactly what had happened between the sailor and, 'some

little shit,' but to be honest I can't say that I really cared that much.

I shook hands with the old sailor. 'Did you hurt him badly?' I inquired.

The man grinned again. 'I hardly touched him Boss,' he laughed. 'He was one

of these young punks who think he is hard.' The old salt laughed again. 'I think

he's changed his mind now,' he explained seriously.

I laughed with him. 'I should think so to,' I agreed.

THE COPPER.

I was on duty one Saturday afternoon when five men were admitted. The first

four were routine. They had all been in custody before.

One of the Prison Officers took me to one side. 'This new lad is rather unusual,' he explained. 'That is why he is last. He will be going straight to the

Segregation Unit.'

'What's the problem?' I inquired.

'He's a policeman,' the officer explained.

The policeman had been called to investigate an allegation of assault by a young

lad. The boy was accused of attacking someone with a metal bar and the bobby

restrained him.

In the police custody suite, the lad stated that he was carrying a gun and made a

threatening gesture. The young copper used force to restrain him and one of his

own colleagues reported him for assault. In court the Judge commented. 'This

was a vulnerable child and you being in a position of trust!' The policeman received a custodial sentence. I gave him the usual interview. I also gave him

the usual advice although in his case the advice was rather more detailed than

usual.

This unfortunate copper spent the night in jail and got bail the next day.

I am a Liverpool lad and proud of the great city which gave me birth. As a point

of pride, I never buy the Sun Newspaper. Many Scousers like myself, boycott

and detest this rag. But one day I happened to pick up an old copy and I read

with interest that this policeman had been released on appeal. On another date I

read an article which explained that he had been reinstated in the police and had

got his old job back.

I was delighted for him.

SOME YEARS LATER.

Some years later I left the Prison Service and was working for the Manchester

Police. One night I was in casual conversation with a plain clothes copper and I

happened to mention Altcourse Jail.

He replied casually. 'I spent the worst night of my life in that place.' He went

on to describe what had happened and I instantly remembered him.

We chatted freely and both of us recalled the incident. He seemed to take relief

from retailing his account of the miscarriage of justice which he had suffered

but I did not have the nerve to inquire if the colleague who had made these

allegations had been disciplined themselves in any way.

In the world in which we currently live that would be far too much to expect.

I felt very sorry for this policeman. I have been in similar positions myself when a so-called 'friend' or colleague with an axe to grind reported me on trumped up charges. Policemen complain that they are faced with 'double jeopardy' in such situations. To explain! This simply means that a police officer can be arrested, go to court, get found not guilty and then is still subject to disciplinary procedures. Even though a jury has acquitted him of any criminal offences he can still be sacked for unprofessional conduct. In plain English he gets tried twice. But at least as a policeman he had the absolute right to know exactly what he is accused of and who is accusing him.

Nurses, of course, are treated differently. They are subject to triple jeopardy.

A nurse can be arrested and found not guilty in a court of law. And, bear in

mind that all of that this can take weeks maybe months. And then, even if they

are found not guilty, they can be called upon to appear before a disciplinary

panel who accuse them of the same offence. It is entirely possible that the

hospital can then decide that even though they have not actually broken the law,

they have acted in an unprofessional manner and sack them anyway. But the

real icing on the cake is that even if they acquitted in court and cleared by the

hospital they can then be called to account by the by the Nursing and Midwifery

Council and face yet another ordeal. They can then be struck off as a nurse and find themselves ruined. And all of this can take many months, sometimes years.

Many years ago, exactly this happened to a friend of mine.

And for good measure I have encountered the situation in nursing on numerous

occasions in nursing when some senior person accuses you of something and

states; 'things have been said.' The Senior then recounts allegations of some

usually trivial or petty matter which may have occurred weeks, perhaps months,

previously and demands a written statement from you. And, when you ask who

has made these allegations you are told. 'Never Mind. That is not the issue.' I

have personally been involved in such situations, as the accused, as a Shop

Steward and as a friend on numerous occasions.

On one occasion a Hospital Administrator demanded written statements from

myself and two care assistants. When we all asked why and asked exactly what

we were accused of he told us, 'things have been said.' Apparently, a violent

female whom we had restrained had 'sustained injuries.' I should point out that

these were bruises to the patient's arms not to her face. In fact, the bruises were

totally consistent with the woman having her arms gripped but a rather peculiar

Doctor had taken it upon himself to, 'say things.' Of course, HE was not asked

for a written statement. We took advice from our union and were advised that in

no circumstances should we make statements until we ourselves had seen copies of the statements of accusation. (These statements did not even exist.) The

Hospital Administrator then informed me that if we refused to make written

statements then he would regard this as, 'a highly suspicious action.'

At the time I was a Shop Steward for the Royal College of Nursing. I asked this

Hospital Administrator exactly what his qualifications were. Apparently, he had

a degree in geophysics. This man had no personal experience, qualifications or

training in medicine, nursing or psychiatry. He had never trained as a

policeman, barrister, lawyer or legal person of any kind. He was neither

qualified, trained nor experienced in Control and Restraint. And yet he took it

upon himself to make judgements like this. Many staff assume that such a person wants to stitch them up in some way and get them sacked or jailed. The

truth is simpler and more prosaic. He just wants written statements so that he

can say to HIS superiors. 'Look at me. I am so clever and conscientious. And

furthermore, I have written statements to prove it.' He does not particularly

want to see me, or anyone else end up sacked, or struck off the Nursing Register

or end up in jail. In fact, he couldn't care less. He is interested in one thing. He

just wants to make himself look good and further his own career.

When I was in management myself, I often encountered this situation when a

staff member would storm into my office in a temper and make allegations

against someone. Of course, if the allegation was of a serious nature then

'YES,' of course, you would investigate. But many times, it was simply petty

trivia which boiled down to, 'I don't like him/her, for whatever reason.'

In such a case then the answer is simple. You shove a piece of paper and a pen

across the desk and invite them to put the allegation in writing. On nearly every

occasion the person stands there looking indignant and surprised then changes

their mind.

This unfortunate copper was, in fact, very lucky. I shook hands with him and

wished him all the best. I have to say though that I would not give much for his

promotion prospects afterwards.

When I was working in Altcourse Jail a colleague grassed me up for writing a

book about the place. I was suspended from work and given an Official

Warning.

In fact, I had informed my superiors in writing THREE TIMES that I

was writing a book about Altcourse.

When I returned to work various people told me, 'in strict confidence,' that my

promotion prospects were now, 'absolutely zero.'

They were right.

THE SCREW.

One evening I was on duty when I received a phone call. It was from a brand-

new, rather inexperienced, young prison officer. 'Can you come and see this lad

please Chris?" he pleaded. 'He says that he is desperately mentally ill and must

see a qualified person immediately.' This officer was a new staff member. Often

the inmate will try and obtain some favour or other which an older screw would

listen politely to and then roar with laughter. In any jail psychiatric nurses

become used to such calls and requests. When you meet the inmate, the

demands vary from the sublime to the ridiculous. Usually the inmate requests

something which you cannot or will not give. It might be a phone call home, a

sick note excusing him from work in the morning, or a transfer to the

Healthcare Unit simply because it is seen as a soft option and they don't like

normal location for any number of reasons. An interesting side issue with

Altcourse Jail at that time was the fact that the Hospital Unit did not have

televisions in the cells. Many a time an inmate, usually a younger lad would

demand admission to the unit and then when he was transferred there, he would

be escorted to the cell at which point he would indignantly shout. 'Where is my

tellie?' When told that hospital cells do not have televisions, he would

immediately and suddenly display a remarkable recovery and demand to be sent

back to normal location.

So, when you get such calls in a prison you sometimes become a bit jaded and the standard response is to tell the officer. 'Look. I am busy. Just put a referral

in and myself or one of my colleagues will see him as soon as possible.' That

evening, just for once I was not busy. I looked at the clock. It was 20.30pm and

my shift finished at 21.30pm. Myself and a group of the girls were sitting round

gossiping in the Hospital Unit. I did not particularly want to attend but in

situations like this I always tried to remember my own golden rule. 'You are

being paid money to do a job,' I told myself. You are not a conscript. You are a

volunteer. So! Do what you are paid money to do.' I told myself that I had over

an hour before my shift finished so I should still get off on time.

By the time I had physically walked across the prison to the Wing, let myself in, met the new, young prison officer, had a handover and then walked up to the

cell to interview the 'desperately ill inmate,' it was 20.20. The clock was

ticking. 'Hello,' I announced. 'My name is Chris. I am a Mental Health Nurse.

You are asking to see to someone. Here I am. What can I do for you?' He was a

young lad, eighteen years old, first time in jail. He had been in custody for less

than a week.

This boy had a wide grin on his face. 'Listen mate,' he gabbled quickly. 'I've

been talking to the lads here. I'm not happy in this jail. I don't like it. I want to

go home. The lads all told me what to say and what to do. So, if I can't go home

then I want to be transferred to a mental hospital. There's one near where I live.

It's where I should be. It's not fair that a boy like me who is mentally ill should

be locked up in jail. It is an abuse of my human rights. And it is your

responsibility to get me out of here and into a good hospital.'

The youngster continued rabbiting on and it was patently obvious that he was

not mentally ill in the slightest. He was simply unhappy.

'You don't go to a Mental Health Hospital because you don't like jail,' I

explained patiently for perhaps the ten thousandth time in my career. 'You go to

hospital because you are mentally ill.'

Just for a moment he looked astounded. He thought for a moment and then

spoke. 'Well I am mentally ill,' he protested quickly.

I sighed. 'What is your mental illness?' I inquired civilly. I was trying to be

polite but even, so I could not help looking at my watch.

The lad thought for a moment. 'I'm an alcoholic,' he stated with a grin. 'I can't

stop drinking so I need to go to hospital where I can receive treatment for my

illness.'

'How the hell can you be an alcoholic in jail?' I asked tersely. 'There is no

booze here.'

The lad looked a bit downcast and thought for a moment. 'Well how about

depression then?' he asked with a wide grin.

'You are not mentally ill,' I explained. 'Your problem is that you don't like

jail.'

I finally finished talking to the boy and put him on the list for an RMN follow

up. We were not abandoning him! He would be seen again by myself, or by one

of my colleagues in the immediate future. Preferably at a time when the RMN

in question had more spare time to listen to his drivel.

Most new prison officers are, as one would expect, a lot more impressionable

than the older more experienced staff and many inmates know this and will try

and manipulate and use new staff members. And many new staff are trained to

always 'cover yourself.' In every way. This usually consists of any possible

problem being referred to someone else. In jail there is an old saying. 'If it is not

written down then it didn't happen.' This statement is written on the walls of many prisons. You can see the logic of it. But this still causes endless trouble

for people like me when we are faced with unrealistic demands and requests

such as this.

I looked at my watch. It was 21.00 exactly. I had to speak to the Prison Officer,

make an entry into his wing file, walk back across the jail, to the Healthcare

Unit, log into the computer, and make a written entry into this boy's file. I was

still hoping to get off on time for a few pints. I was just finishing a fourteen-

hour shift and, with the best will in the world we all get tired.

I explained matters to the young prison officer, and he listened impatiently as I

informed him of my actions and decisions.

'Listen!' the screw asked me. 'Before you go can you see his mate as well? He is in the next cell and he has just told me that he desperately needs to see you as well.'

'Jesus Christ,' I inwardly groaned to myself. 'What did I do in a previous life to deserve this?'

I gave a weary nod of acquiescence and opened the adjoining cell.

The lad in this cell greeted me cheerfully. 'Alright mate,' he said with a wide grin on his face. 'Listen mate if my pal is going to a mental hospital then I want to go as well. I want to be sectioned and taken to hospital.' He grinned again.

'You see I am mentally ill as well. Alright mate?' (Section or sectioned; this simply means being forcibly taken into a Mental Health Hospital.)

'You can't be sectioned if you want to go to a mental Hospital,' I explained.

'People are only sectioned if they are unwilling.'

'But I am mentally ill.' He protested.

I gave another inward groan 'What is your illness?' I asked wearily.

'I'm an alcoholic,' he proclaimed triumphantly. He and his mate had obviously

been discussing what tactics to use.

'How can you be an alcoholic in here? I asked. 'You can't drink alcohol in jail.'

His face fell. 'Well I've got schizophrenia,' he announced.

'Tell me all about your schizophrenia?' I asked.

'What do you mean?'

'Well what are the signs and symptoms of this illness? What are the problems

that it causes you?'

He looked at me for another long moment as he tried to think. He was obviously

not used to this and he was finding this new procedure difficult and painful. 'I

think that I am two different people,' he claimed tentatively.

(Everyone in the Western World has seen the film or read the book about Jekyll

and Hyde the 'split personality,' who was two totally different characters at

different times. When inmates claim that they feel like two different people then

you can guarantee they are telling lies. I worked in psychiatry for over thirty

years and not once ever did I ever meet a GENUINE 'split personality.' And,

contrary to popular opinion, schizophrenia is nothing to do with this semi-

mythical mental illness anyway.)

'So, what problems does this cause you?' I inquired.

'Well I hear voices Boss,' he stated more confidently.

'What time of day do you hear these voices?' I asked.

He looked at me for a moment and then spoke. 'First thing of a morning,' he

suggested tentatively.

In schizophrenia people usually hear the voices at any hour of the day or night.

But the last thing you ever do with inmates is to give them, answers or

knowledge.

'First thing of a morning?' I queried.

'That's right mate,' he agreed gratefully. 'I always hear the voices first thing of

a morning.'

'Where do the voices come from?' I inquired.

Again, the lad looked closely at me and then glanced around for inspiration. He

was obviously trying to work out the correct answer. 'From inside my head,' he

suggested nervously.

In schizophrenia voices can come from everywhere, but the doctor or nurse

should never volunteer information in cases like this.

'From inside your head?' I commented in a deadpan voice.

He grinned again. 'That's right mate,' he agreed with a big grin. 'The voices

always come from inside my head.'

'Are they male or female voices?' I asked.

Once more he looked searchingly at me. 'They are both male and female voices,' he replied cautiously.

In schizophrenia the voices are usually male.

I gave a big grin as if I was agreeing with him. 'Are you sure of that?' I

inquired.

He gave a big grin. 'That's right mate,' he announced. 'The voices I hear are

always male and female.'

In a psychotic mental illness, the voices are usually strident male voices which

speak about the person in a derogatory manner and appear to come from above

his head.

This stupid conversation continued for about twenty minutes and not once did

he get one single answer right.

I looked at my watch again. I will put you down for an RMN follow up,' I told him.

The lad looked amazed and angry. 'What does that mean?' he asked.

'It means that one of my colleagues or myself will come and see you at some time in the future when he has more time than I have now,' I explained patiently.

'Well when will that be?' he asked impatiently.

'I honestly don't know,' I explained. 'It depends how many people are on the list already. It could be tomorrow. It could be next week.'

The boy looked even more annoyed. 'You don't seem to understand,' he claimed aggressively. 'I want to go a hospital. Me and my mate both want to go. And we want to go right now. Not tomorrow or next week. We want to go right now. Alright?'

'Look you silly, little boy,' I explained. 'The chances of you going to a mental

hospital is not nil. They are less than nil. You are no more mentally ill than I

am.'

'I am mentally ill,' he protested faintly.

I looked at him in sheer and utter exasperation. 'So am I,' I replied. I looked at

my watch. I was going to be late getting home.

I did make it in time for my last pint that night.

Some people will be appalled and horrified at stories like this but what else

could myself and other staff do?

During conversations with inmates, you always ask 'open-ended,' questions such as the ones I have described. In that way the patient must answer the

questions himself rather than in just agreeing with whatever it is that you say.

Incidentally! What are the chances of getting such a boy into a mental hospital?

'It would be easier to get a boy about into Eton.'

That is a word for word quote from Professor Anthony Maden who is a

professor of Forensic Psychiatry.

The next time that I was on duty with that Prison Officer I made a point of

having a conversation with him in which I explained the realities and difficulties

of getting anyone admitted to a mental hospital. I also explained that I could

quite understand why he had taken the actions which he did. I tried hard not to criticise him or diminish him in any way. The very last thing I wanted was to

lower his self-esteem in any way. I just asked him to be more careful in future.

To be fair the Prison Officer listened carefully and thanked me for the advice.

He never did that again.

THE DOCTOR.

In my career I worked with people of every conceivable race, religion, colour

and sexuality. I trained in nursing in the British Health Service. This is an

institution to be proud of. It is admired and respected the world over. Long

before the modern, politically correct obsession with, 'human rights' the Health

Service always refused to discriminate against people who were Black, Asian, gay or disabled. Such people have made a tremendous contribution, not just to

medicine and nursing, but to British culture. And I have always admired people

who travelled the world to make a new life for themselves and who have given

so generously of their talents to this country. Every so often, though you meet

someone who contradicts the preconceived ideas of fair play, honesty and

integrity which we all subconsciously give to our foreign friends.

Many foreign Doctors speak our language well, but their grammar is limited to

'Oxford English.' Yet a psychiatrist must understand a patient's background,

culture and language or else how can he assess and understand his problems.

Much less prescribe treatment.

A MENTAL HOSPITAL.

MANY YEARS AGO.

I was once asked to accompany a new doctor on his first interview. Another,

older Doctor who introduced us told his friend. 'The local language here in

Liverpool is called Scouse. Fortunately for us Chris speaks this language

fluently so he can translate for you.'

I didn't know whether to laugh or not.

I was with this Doctor when he interviewed a young, Irish patient and I

listened afterwards as he explained the problems of this lad. According to this

doctor the patient was speaking a foreign language and had difficulty in

understanding English language. I informed him that the Irish speak English as

their first language.

The Doctor disagreed. 'Ever since the rebellion of 1916 when Ireland became independent the Irish now speak their own language,' he explained condescendingly.

'No, they don't,' I informed him. 'The Irish speak English. Only a tiny percentage of them can even speak Irish.'

He became angry. 'How would you know?' he asked. 'Have you ever been to Ireland?'

'I've been to Ireland lots of times,' I explained. 'As a matter of fact, my family are Irish.'

'In that case your family are upper-class English Protestants,' he asserted wrongly. 'You have the typical English prejudices.'

'My family are working class Irish Catholics,' I pointed out. 'And I am not in the slightest bit prejudiced.'

'If you are Roman Catholic then you must sympathise with organisations such as the IRA,' this doctor accused me.

Sometimes when you meet people from a totally different cultural background who make value judgements because of their own education and from there, own experiences it is difficult to have rational conversations with them.

'I have no sympathy at all for the IRA,' I replied truthfully. 'I am British and I support the British Army one hundred per cent. And I am not prejudiced in the least.'

'Yes, you are,' this man shouted. 'You were obviously educated by English schoolteachers, so you have been brainwashed to believe this rubbish about

Ireland.'

As a matter fact I was educated by Irish, Christian Brothers at St Anselm's

College on the Wirral, but I didn't bother telling him this. There is an old

saying. 'You can't argue with blind prejudice.'

Sometimes this Asian Doctor worked with staff of similar ethnic origins. They

had an extremely annoying habit of talking together in their own

incomprehensible dialect in front of both staff and patients. As politely as I

could I have explained to this gentleman that this is extremely bad manners. I also pointed out that if a person is paranoid then they may get upset because

they think that you are talking about them and this will make them worse.

He got very indignant and accused ME of doing the same thing.

'You talk Scouse to the staff and patients in front of myself and other staff,' he

accused me. 'We cannot understand what you are saying.'

I thought for a moment. In this Liverpool hospital prior to this, four Welsh

Students had a habit of talking to each other in Welsh. The Ward Sister

called them into the office and told them to cease this practise.

'I can speak my own language in my own country,' one of them replied nastily.

'Yes!' the Sister agreed emphatically. 'But you are not in your own country. As a matter of fact you are in England. Not Wales.'

They had no answer to that.

When the doctor accused me of talking Scouse to people, I remembered this

conversation. 'I am in Liverpool,' I pointed out. 'So, if I want to talk Scouse to

Scousers then that is my privilege.' I grinned at him. 'If ever I work in your

country then I will not speak English to English people while on duty,' I

promised. 'Nor will I talk Scouse to Scousers.'

IN PRISON.

In Jail I was asked to accompany another doctor and I had a real sense of déjà

vu when I encountered a situation in a Liverpool Prison years later. This prisoner was a rough, working-class Liverpool lad from the backstreets of

Toxteth. He sat facing the Doctor and spoke at length.

'Well ya' know the score Boss. What 'appenned was this. Me an' me mate went

t' th' boozer an' we was paralytic! Out t' game! Well oiled! On the way 'ome

me an me mate wus' goin' down a back jigger and got into a barney wit' sum

geezer, oo' was comin' the cunt. I nutted 'im. But 'e wellied me back so I

bottled the bastard. The scuffers cum' so I done a runner. I 'ad bad previous an'

I went on me' toes. But sum' bastard grassed me up. I got me collar felt an' was

bang to rights. Put me 'ands up to it. Got weighed off and went down the steps.

I got 'alf a stretch. (five years) I was well pissed off. But I'm in a good nick.

Decent screws 'ere, not like some places. Dead chuffed about that. An' the cons

'ere are sound. No nonces anyway.'

I tried not to laugh as I translated. The Doctor thanked me courteously.

This new Doctor seemed to fit in well. Prison Staff must be broad minded and

easy going.

But one day another new doctor arrived, and he was rather unusual. Someone

mentioned a holiday in Malta, and he became very angry and upset. He

described the Knights Templars of Malta who had raided the coasts of peace

loving, Muslim countries and murdered and raped Muslims. All of this occurred

over a thousand years ago, but this doctor spoke as if it were yesterday.

I listened in fascination.

This doctor reminded me of another man whom I had once met. This was a

member of the National Front. Another fanatic who also lectured me at length.

His theory though, was about the Black/Jewish/Zionist conspiracy to take over

the world.

I remember listening to him as well.

I have had to listen to an awful lot of rubbish in my time.

Both these two fanatics were highly intelligent, and both men had beliefs that

bordered on stupidity, in fact almost insanity. But, contrary to popular opinion it

is perfectly possible to be intelligent and have stupid beliefs. The Nazis and the

Communists for instance fulfil these conditions admirably.

This Doctor was not even Asian. He was British born but seemed to bear an

abiding dislike of Great Britain.

Again, I was, and still am, amazed. 'Let me ask you a question?' I replied. 'If

we had an Islamic fundamentalist in this place would you treat him the same as

everyone else?'

The Doctors' eyes clouded over, and he regarded me suspiciously. 'That is a

completely different matter,' he answered. 'You have to understand why we

Muslims are fighting in the first place. We have been persecuted by the Great

Satan (United States) and the little Satan. (Great Britain). These men who you

Term, 'Islamic Fundamentalists' are not criminals or terrorists at all. They are brave, freedom fighters who are trying to defeat the western conspiracy which

wants to destroy and pollute the Muslim religion.'

SOME WEEKS LATER.

I seriously wondered what to do about this man.

In the end I completed an SIR which detailed our conversations and I explained

that I regarded this Doctor as a serious security risk as his sympathies obviously

lay with extremist, Islamic fundamentalists.

Not long afterwards he was told that we no longer required his services.

The expression, 'good riddance to bad rubbish,' springs to mind.

In the prison service we have an overriding responsibility to our duty.

Our duty is to the British public and to the Prison Service.

THE NURSE.

When I worked in Altcourse Prison one of the many home truths which were

quickly made apparent to me was the simple fact that private enterprise is

interested in one thing, and one thing only. Making money! The whole concept

of making money out of locking people up is morally wrong. Any one of my

age group, and I was born in the 1950's, well remembers the stupidity of the

Trade Union movements of those days which brought down governments and

enforced ridiculous and expensive restrictive practices on industry. In all fairness some managers were even more stupid. The combination of stupid

management and equally stupid trade unions led to the demise of British

industry from which it has never recovered.

My Line Manager in Altcourse was a woman who loved the concept of saving

money. She thought that this made her look good to her bosses. One of her more

ridiculous schemes were to try and enforce a rule that ONE nurse was enough to

staff the hospital wing in the prison. The logic behind her judgement was clear.

The fewer members of staff employed then the more money she saved and the

better she looked as a manager. Many people, including myself, protested

vigorously at this decision. Many of the female staff pointed out that the prospect was a frightening one. Suppose an inmate suddenly grabbed the staff

member and overpowered them. A male nurse could be assaulted maybe

murdered. A dangerous criminal could overpower him, steal his uniform and

Security Pass and escape. A female nurse could be raped. And why? To save

money.

The Manager gave us her answer. 'If you are attacked simply press your First

Response button.'

This advice sound great but it totally ignores the reality of what happens if a

couple of big, strong inmates suddenly jump a staff member.

One day I drew the short straw and was ordered to manage the Healthcare

Ward. I didn't really mind. There was one single patient on the ward that day and he was a small, slightly built man about five-foot five inches tall. He

approached me. 'Excuse me Boss?' he asked politely. 'If you are not busy could

you get me a towel please?'

'Sure!' I acknowledged. I got the man a towel and he thanked me politely. 'No

problems,' I thought and went back to reading my book. I like reading and when

the hospital unit was quiet it was understood that so long as any necessary work

was completed then staff could read books, play computer games or watch

television. I once listened while a senior man explain that in such circumstances

staff should engage with inmates and give them activities to participate in. Once

again this is the type of rubbish constantly peddled by senior people with no first-hand experience of jail. How in God's name could I spend an entire shift of

seven and a half hours in talking to one unfortunate inmate who just wanted to

be left alone?

One of my colleagues who I worked with in Altcourse Jail was another RMN

named Dave. I myself am about five foot eleven and weigh about thirteen

stone. Dave is a couple of inches taller than me, a stone or so heavier and ten

years younger. We are both well trained and experienced in Control and

Restraint.

Dave wandered into the unit that day and spoke politely to the one sole inmate.

Just like me he was always polite to inmates. This is not psychiatry. It is just

common sense. 'How are you?' he inquired civilly.

The man looked at him with a deadpan expression for about three seconds and

then erupted. 'How am I?' he screamed at the top of his voice. 'How am I? I'll

tell you how I am! I'm insane! I'm fucking mad! Fuck off you bastard!'

The man violently threw the TV control straight at Dave's face and then

physically attacked him.

Dave and I are both big lads and both of us are well experienced in violence, but

this was a classic even for us.

We grabbed the little man and it was like restraining a snake. He writhed,

wriggled and twisted like a slimy eel. We finally managed to get arm locks on

him. He lunged forward and tried to bite my face. With my right hand I was

holding his left arm as Dave grabbed his right arm. The man was still fighting furiously and, once again he tried to bite me. I kneed him in the stomach,

grabbed his throat with my left hand and shoved his head backwards.

At that exact moment our Line Manager walked in. The First Response Team

was not far behind. Gratefully we handed the man over to them. He was

escorted to the Segregation Unit and that was the last we saw of him.

We never bothered, 'nicking' him. I personally thought he was quite insane. I

think my colleague agreed with me.

TEN MINUTES LATER.

The Manager faced me, and I could see that she was angry. 'Just what the

bloody hell did you think you were doing?' she inquired calmly and with an

expression of cold anger on her face.

At the time I could not understand why she was so angry. 'That man attacked

Dave,' I explained. 'He is raving bloody mad. We had to restrain him. He

attacked both of us.'

'When I walked in there you were strangling him,' she accused me. 'You had

your hands around his throat and you were choking him. Is that what you call,

'Control and Restraint?' This situation has happened to me on many occasions

both in hospitals and in prisons. A violent situation occurs, and a senior person

arrives. And is Murphy's Law that by the time they arrive it is always after the

real violence has been dealt with. All that the senior person sees is the restraint

and then they are very quick to criticise the people involved. Mind you if they personally, are involved in a violent situation then, 'that is different.' If that

happens then the senior person will then go around the workplace telling

everyone they meet in the most lurid and graphic terms imaginable how the

patient or inmate, 'tried to kill me.'

I didn't exaggerate. I simply told the truth.

It's a bad habit of mine.

'That man tried to bite me,' I explained. 'I had to grab his throat to stop him.

I had no choice in the matter.'

I produced my watch which had been damaged in the affray. 'My watch is

broken,' I pointed out. 'Can I have a Claims Form for a repair?'

She looked straight at me. 'No, you cannot,' she snarled. 'If your watch is broken then that is an occupational hazard. It is nothing to do with the Prison.'

'But I am entitled for compensation for damage to my property,' I protested.

'You are wrong on that issue,' she snarled. 'And count yourself lucky that I am

not reporting the pair of you for excessive force and brutality.'

The woman refused to discuss the matter any further. She stormed off. At the

time I could not understand why she was so angry. It was only later that day

when I heard the girls gossiping that I realised why she was so angry.

Every one of the girls was repeating the same refrain. 'Chris and Dave are two

big lads, both well trained in restraint and there was ONE single patient on the

Hospital Unit at that time. And one inmate attacked the two of them. Imagine if it had been one of us? Imagine one, small female on her own? What would have

happened then?' Of course, the Manger had no answer to this. So, like many

inadequate people she took refuge in getting angry.

There is an old saying in psychiatry. 'Unreasoning anger is always based on a

negative emotion.' The negative emotion is usually fear although it may be

guilt, jealousy, envy or in this case sheer bloody mindedness because she

thought that she had been made to look stupid. In this instance just for once, she

was totally right. She had been made to look stupid.

So, I could well understand why she was so angry. Nevertheless, I was

determined that my watch was going to be repaired. I left it a couple of hours so that she could calm down and then walked into her office again. 'Look,' I

explained. 'I want to claim for my watch being broken. Can I have a Claims

Form for it please?'

Far from calming down she appeared even angrier. 'Your watch being

broken is an occupational hazard,' she shouted. 'And count yourself lucky that

you are not being disciplined for using excessive force. I have answered this

question twice. I am not answering it again. Now get out of my office and stop

pestering me. I am busy.'

'You would think that she was paying for the bloody watch herself,' I thought.

'Look,' I explained. 'Just give me a Claim Form please. If the company refuses

to pay me, you have lost nothing.'

'No, I will not give you a Claims Form,' she stormed at me. 'Now will you get

out of my office.'

I was rather annoyed at this. I got my watch repaired and collected a receipt. I

sent this with a covering letter to HER Line Manager and, without any quibble

he sent me a cheque for £38 for my watch repair.

Moral of the story. 'If the Manger likes you then you can do no wrong. If she

does not like you then you can do no right.'

Maybe I should have just toed the line and kept my head down and told this

manager whatever it is that she wanted to hear and spent my life grassing up

other staff members like certain other people did.

But I have never been very good at any of those things.

THE IRISHMAN.

Sometimes working in a High Security prison, you meet men whom you do feel

sorry for. Sometimes though you meet a person whose behaviour has been so

stupid that it is difficult to feel any emotion other than pure and utter

amazement at the stupidity of their behaviour. Most British people dislike the

Provisional IRA intensely. And most people, British, Irish or Outer Mongolian,

know very well that it is not wise to get on the wrong side of this organisation.

A man came through Admissions. An Irishman, obviously hailing from the

Republic. Northern and Southern Irish accents are very distinctive and are an

immediate giveaway.

'What are you in for?' I asked casually.

He started talking and his answers were, quite literally, mind boggling.

Apparently, he knew of an IRA arms dump on the Irish Border. So, he stole

three, Russian-made, Baikal pistols, three silencers and several hundred rounds

of ammunition. His plan was to smuggle this equipment into Britain where he

would sell it to criminals.

I looked at him incredulously. 'How much would you have got for three

automatic pistols?' I asked in genuine curiosity.

'About two or three hundred pounds apiece,' he answered slowly.

'So, what exactly happened?' I inquired.

'Well I got off the boat at Holyhead,' he explained. 'And the Special Branch where waiting for me. They turned the car inside out and found all the guns and

ammo.' The man paused. 'To be honest I think someone must have tipped them

off. I tried bluffing it out. I said I had never even seen these guns before, but it

didn't work. My fingerprints were all over them.'

'They probably were tipped off,' I agreed. 'The IRA don't like people who

steal guns from them.'

'So, in addition to a long jail sentence I have also got an IRA Hit Contract out

on me,' he complained.

'Have you seen a brief?' I asked.

'Yeah,' he replied. 'He told me that nowadays I would automatically get five

years for any firearms offence but in this case, I will get at least ten years.

Possibly fifteen or twenty depending on the judge.'

I have met some stupid criminals in my time. And I take great exception when

people describe the Irish as stupid. I am of Irish extraction myself. But this man

was in a class of his own.

To be facing ten or fifteen years in jail was bad enough. And he had no possible

defence. Any judge would give long sentences in such circumstances. And the

IRA has a long memory. And he would be serving his stretch in High Security

prisons which hold IRA and INLA men. And when released he would be facing

death or possibly kneecapping. Or even worse. People who have annoyed the

IRA have disappeared and their bodies never even been found. It is generally believed that if a man has been brutally tortured then the Provisionals will not

want the body discovered.

And to be facing all of this for a total of perhaps a thousand pounds at most!

The word stupidity is the year's masterpiece of understatement.

I sometimes wonder if he is still alive.

THE ULSTERMAN.

The entrance to any Wing in Altcourse Prison is a large, gated, grilled door

which gives out onto a spacious area dominated by the console. This is simply a

big desk sited on top of a small platform. It is equipped with telephones and

other office equipment. To one side is the dining area and this is open plan. I found myself one day chatting in an informal manner to a gang of particularly,

obnoxious young inmates who were boasting and bragging to me all about their

criminal careers. They were all members of a couple of infamous Liverpool

Street Gangs, the Crocs and the Dogs. They had all committed numerous crimes

and were proud and pleased to tell me all about their activities. This may sound

incredible to the ordinary person but what else can crooks talk about. And, since

an awful lot of them spend most of their lives in jail what else can they discuss

other than crime and prison. This little gang were rabbiting on about crimes

which they had been involved in. Or rather the crimes which they claimed to

have been involved in. Prisoners often exaggerate and brag about their activities. I have known a man boast that he was charged with armed robbery

when really, he was in jail for shoplifting. At great length they discoursed about

theft and housebreaking, guns and shootings, beatings and violence, drugs and

robberies, crime and criminals.

Standing there, listening patiently, was a very tall, well-built Ulsterman. His

face had a completely deadpan expression as he listened to these little boys.

This Irishman was about six foot four inches tall and broad built with it. He had

fists like sledgehammers and the muscles of a professional weightlifter. I had

met him quite a few times and whenever we conversed, he was always softly

spoken, polite and courteous. On one occasion he asked me my name and when

I introduced myself, he gave a surprised grimace. Quite calmly he said to me.

'Are you a Taig Boss? (Taig: Northern Ireland slang for a Roman Catholic. I

have an Irish Catholic name so he was correct in this assumption.) When I told

him he was right, he laughed and introduced me to his pad-mate who was also

from Northern Ireland. It transpired that the big man was an Ulsterman who was

an ex-member of the UFV. (Ulster Volunteer Force an illegal, Protestant, para-

military organisation) His friend and cell mate were, an ex-member of the

Provisional IRA. Some pair!

The two men were standing there listening to these youngsters and, finally, the

big Protestant turned to me. 'Tell me Boss? How long do you reckon these boyoes would have lasted in the old days down the Shankhill or the Falls?' he

asked politely.

'About five minutes,' I guessed, 'if they were very lucky.'

(NB the Shankhill Rd was one of the toughest Protestant ghettoes in Northern

Ireland in the days of 'the Troubles.' The Falls Rd was an equally tough

Catholic area which bordered it and some of the bitterest and most intense

rioting and killings ever seen in Britain took place there. They were divided by

the Peace Line which was a thirty-foot tall fence specially erected to stop the

two sides from killing each other.)

One of these little boys faced the big Irishman. 'Do you know who we are?' he

asked arrogantly. 'We run the drugs in Croxteth,' he boasted. 'Me and my mates aint' scared of no one. We aint' scared of nobody, nor nuffin.'

Quite calmly, without any apparent effort, in fact without even quickening his breathing, the big Ulsterman gripped the boy around the throat, picked him clear off the ground and held him up against a wall.

The boy's face changed colour from a dirty, spotty-faced, acne-coated white to a deep purple. 'Are you speaking to me sonny-boy?' the big man inquired politely.

The reply was an incoherent, strangled sob.

Gently, very gently the big Ulsterman placed the little boy back on the ground and turned back to me. 'I think you are wrong Boss,' he remarked calmly. 'I do not think any of these kids would have lasted five minutes in the old days in

Belfast or Londonderry.'

I couldn't help it. I just burst out laughing.

There were three or four ODCs (O.D.C.s Ordinary Decent Criminals.) and a

couple of screws standing there. They all burst out laughing as well.

The big Protestant turned to me. 'Nice meeting you, Boss,' he commented

politely. 'Take care.' He shook hands with me politely and walked off.

I started laughing again.

The little boy looked distinctly upset.

He turned to me in amazement and surprise. 'Are you going to let him get away

with that mate?' he shouted indignantly.

I gave the boy back, stare for stare. 'Listen to me,' I explained patiently. 'You

are in jail now. You are not in school anymore. I would suggest that you stop showing off and behave yourself.

And, incidentally,' I emphasised. 'Don't call me mate. My mates all wear grey

shirts.'

THE LADY!

I sat chatting cheerfully to one young lad. He was quite friendly and open. As

always, the talk was about crime and criminals. He was from a small, provincial

town and he and his mates were all relaxed in my presence. It is quite sad to

relate that many such boys must come into custody before they ever meet a

stable male role model in their lives. I had the experience of young lads

being admitted to Altcourse Prison and asking for me by name. We were chatting about pubs, clubs, drinking, and of course crime, when, at some point,

in the conversation I asked casually. 'What do you do in your spare time?

Where do you go of a day and of a night?'

'Well during the day, we hang around the one-armed bandit arcades or do a bit

of shoplifting,' he explained. 'Or we steal a few cans of beer and go to the local

park. We smoke drugs in the Park Shelter. If someone's mum is out, then we go

around, to her house, play music and smoke weed or heroin. Of a night we steal

cars and go joy riding. Or we do a bit of housebreaking. If we have any money,

we go to a club I know. We have a couple of beers there. See the lads.

Have a bit of a laugh. You know.'

This last bit of the talk sounded reasonable. Vaguely I visualised a gang of young boys chatting in a friendly manner. Maybe a game of darts. Perhaps

snooker or billiards, a few pints. Chatting about girls, booze, football, gambling;

all the things that young lads love to talk about.

'My mother works there,' he elaborated. 'She is a real lady. All my mates fancy

her.'

'Oh, is she the barmaid?' I enquired.

'No,' he answered casually. 'My mum and her mate work there. Me and me

pals go there to watch them doing naked, lesbian, mud wrestling together.'

Well. I have heard some conversation stoppers in my time but that one really

took the biscuit.

Possibly, just for once, my face gave away some of what I was thinking. 'My

mum is a real lady,' he protested.

Many years ago, when working in psychiatry, I made myself a serious promise.

I said to myself. 'When I am no longer disgusted, I will resign from this job.'

I started work as a Mental Health Nurse in 1977. I retired from that job

after more than thirty years working with the warped dregs of humanity.

And yes! Even after more than thirty years I still found myself being disgusted.

But on balance in this instance I can't pretend that I was really THAT disgusted.

In retrospect it was just a funny story. In the job I worked in you developed a

funny sense of humour. If you didn't then you go mad.

I stood up and picked up my notebook and pen. I did not bother to shake hands

with him. I just said. 'Well it's been nice meeting you,' I stated cheerfully. 'I'll

see you again some time.'

I didn't bother.

THE GENTLEMAN.

I met one man who came into jail charged with murder. Apparently, his wife

had a terminal illness and he quietly, gently and sorrowfully helped her out of

her pain and misery. He then made a very serious suicide attempt. Unbelievably

he lived. He was an old age pensioner at the time. A tall, handsome, charming

man, who had served his country with loyalty and honour in the Armed Forces.

When I met him, he was extremely courteous? He talked in a polite and rational

manner and was sorrowful about his wife but obviously did not regret his

actions. On one occasion he asked me if I was married. I explained politely but

curtly that I was also widowed. He looked at me closely but never pursued the

matter. He obviously had good manners.

Something that is in very short supply nowadays.

Although I personally had a great deal of sympathy for him, I did not believe he

was mentally ill in the slightest.

Finally, I was told that the old chap was going to be transferred to a Mental

Health Unit and that I was to escort him. On the day of his transfer I entered the

Enhanced Wing and the old gentleman approached me. He snapped to attention, clicked his heels and informed me that he was, 'Ready to go Sir.'

Normally we used a sweat box (An armoured security van) for transfers, but

someone, somewhere, with some humanity had decided, that, in this case, a car

would be good enough.

'We are not going to handcuff you,' I explained. 'I don't think you will try and

run away.'

'I give you my word of honour Sir that I will not try and escape,' the old man

promised me seriously. Incidentally if he had managed to escape then both

myself and my prison colleagues would have been looking for new jobs. The

old chap stood smartly to attention and we waited patiently as various staff and

inmates approached him. They all shook hands and wished him the best of luck.

The old chap kept on inspecting his own feet and I could not help but look as

well. He was immaculately dressed in a smart shirt and tie, starched collar,

tweed jacket and flannel trousers. I found myself staring at his brand-new

trainers. This just seemed incongruous. The old gentleman explained.

Apparently, the other inmates approached him that morning and informed him

that they had conducted a whip round and bought him the trainers as a leaving

present. 'The criminals on this wing are actually quite a decent bunch of chaps

Sir,' the old gentleman informed me.

He went on to explain that, that morning at breakfast one young lad approached

him and took his cornflakes off him. The old man was somewhat annoyed but also surprised at this as the other lads on the wing had always been so decent to

him. The young boy then gave him a plate of muesli and shook hands with him.

'You can have my muesli Dad,' the youngster told him. 'I've got nothing else to

give you so take this from me and the best of luck to you.'

'I was quite touched,' the old man informed me.

So was I.

The gentleman then laughed and told me. 'To be honest Sir I don't even like

muesli.'

FOUR HOURS LATER.

After we had dropped the old gentleman off at the hospital, we stopped for a fry

up breakfast and scoffed greedily. One of the prison officers turned to me. 'Tell me something Chris,' the man requested. 'You have been working in psychiatry

for years. You spent three hours chatting to that old guy on the way here. I am

not trained in psychiatry like you. But tell me. Is he mentally ill?'

I smiled. 'Not in the slightest,' I answered.

'Then why has he been transferred to a Mental Health Unit?' the screw asked.

I smiled again. 'The old guy is a political disaster,' I explained. 'He cannot be

seen to be getting away with killing his wife. We are not talking shoplifting. We

are talking murder or manslaughter. But he is an old man, who has served his

country. If he is sentenced to life imprisonment for murder, there would be a

public outcry. So, he gets sectioned and taken into a psychiatric hospital. That

way everyone is happy.'

I heard later that the old man was found not guilty of murder. The likelihood of

his offending again was nil. His previous excellent character was taken into

consideration. He was given a conditional discharge for manslaughter on the

grounds of diminished responsibility.

Maybe there is something to be said for British Justice after all.

THE NONCE.

This was another old soldier. He was a big, broad-shouldered individual with

the muscles of an all-in wrestler and a badly battered face. He was in his mid-

thirties and although he had been discharged from the army years previously, he

still looked and walked like a soldier. Unlike many ex-servicemen he never discussed his army service, but I knew that he had served many years in tough

regiments had and done time in Afghanistan and the Middle East. He was

accused of sexually molesting little boys and girls with great brutality. One

allegation was of actual penetration of a small girl. He claimed he was

innocent.

On admission he was offered Rule 43, but he declined. In conversation with

other cons he remained taciturn and non-committal about himself and his

alleged crimes but, nevertheless, as always happens in a closed community the

truth leaked out. There are many ways in which this can happen. Prisoners often

accompany each other to court and may well sit downstairs of the courtroom while a trail is being conducted upstairs. Many cases are reported in the media

and cons in jail follow all cases avidly. An inmate may have friends from the

same area as the accused who knows details of the crimes. Staff are human and

just like all people they talk. Inmates are always keen listeners for any juicy

piece of gossip.

The Wing Manager took the man to one side and strongly suggested that he

should move on to the Protection Wing. Again, he refused. Very few prison

staff have any sympathy whatever for sex offenders (Although I have known it.)

but the reasons why staff want to get rid of such men are pragmatic not

charitable. No manager or senior staff wants a bashing, knifing or, worst case scenario, a murder, on their wing. (It looks bad when you go for promotion.)

Several days went by with no apparent trouble and the officers relaxed slightly.

'Maybe everything would be alright after all,' they reasoned to themselves.

However, one young lad fancied making a name for himself. He picked his time

and place carefully. At dinner time on the wing with dozens of cons milling

around the youngster suddenly stood right in front of the soldier. For no reason

he squared up to the sex offender and called him a nonce. As he did this the

young lad looked all around to make sure that there were plenty of witness'.

When I spoke to the young fellow afterwards, I got the full story. 'It was only a

joke Boss,' this stripling expostulated. Apparently, he expected the other inmates to join in on his side if any actual violence started. They didn't.

Unfortunately for the young lad this the soldier had no sense of humour. He

immediately kicked the lad in the testicles, then as he doubled up in agony,

kicked him in the face.

The kid was catapulted backwards and collapsed in a puddle of blood. Not one

single con spoke, although many continued eating their dinner. The soldier

turned to the nearest screw and held his hands out in submission. 'Better nick

me, Boss,' he suggested tonelessly.

The officer nicked him. In front of the visiting magistrate the soldier swore that

this kid had repeatedly threatened him and threatened to kill him. The soldier

insisted that on the day of the fracas the kid had accosted him earlier on, boasted that he had a knife and threatened to kill him. There were no witnesses to this.

In fact, there were no witness' to any of the trouble apart from the two prison

officers who had only witnessed the actual assault. (It could not be called a

fight.)

The kid swore that the soldier had threatened him and promised to kill him and

then attacked him for no reason at all.

I don't know who the magistrate believed but the soldier got four weeks in jail.

And after that little episode no one went near him.

One day I was chatting to an old con who pointed the ex-soldier out and told

me. 'He's in for messing around with children Boss, but I don't believe a word

of it. He's a decent guy. He wouldn't do a thing like that.'

The fact that he was a big, rough, tough, six-foot, fourteen-stone bruiser who

had been trained in unarmed combat was of course, totally irrelevant.

THE GRASS.

One day I was completing a medicine round when a man approached me,

accepted his capsules and then appeared to accidentally drop some of them onto

the floor. He politely handed me them back, and, just as politely asked me for

some fresh tablets. I issued him with new medication to replace the ones he had

dropped on the floor and thought nothing more of it.

An hour or so later I was sitting at a wing table completing some notes when another man approached me. 'Can I have a word with you please Boss?' he

inquired.

This is a quite normal request. Prisoners live a very claustrophobic life and

every visitor to the wing is instantly weighed up by the prisoners. Someone will

know who you are and what your job is. The man who approached me that day

was a tall, skinny, smelly youngster wearing unwashed, ragged clothes. He had

old track marks down both arms. He was ugly, with an angular, unshaven face

and crafty, alert eyes.

When I got to know him, I realised that he was one of the most unpleasant

individuals I have ever encountered.

And, that really is saying something.

'What can I do for you? I asked civilly.

The young man grinned. He sat facing me and gave an unpleasant leer. Unlike

many inmates he had none of the flashy, ostentatious jewellery that personifies

the man who regards himself as a successful crook. Many such people love to

show off. But this boy just looked like a tramp.

'My name is Paul,' he introduced himself. 'When you were giving the

medication out this morning my mate dropped his capsules. And you gave him

some new ones. That is a regular trick of his. He has some old capsules palmed

in his hand and he has cut them open to take the chemicals out. He then glues

them back together and swallows the stuff from the new capsules that he has

dropped on the floor.'

'Jesus Christ,' I swore. 'I was amazed. Not just at the lengths which inmates are

prepared to go to steal tiny amounts of medication but also at the pathetic lives

they must lead. I informed the other staff about this new trick and thought no

more of it.

The next time I visited that wing the scruffy grass approached me again. He

named another inmate and gave me his cell number. 'He is brewing hooch in

there, Boss,' he promised. 'Under his bed he has a polythene, lemonade carton

filled full of orange juice mixed with bread. His mate (the grass named the

friend as well) has stolen some yeast from the kitchen and they are brewing it

all up together.' Bread and yeast mixed with orange juice will ferment together and produce a nauseating mixture that inmates get high on.

I passed this information on and, again it was perfectly true.

Another time Paul approached me. 'Don't look round now Boss,' he told me.

'But there are three lads sitting to together behind you. One of them has got

short brown hair. His girlfriend keeps on sending him pornographic

photographs of herself. Behind the stamps on each letter there is some heroin.

The theory is that the staff will be so fascinated by the porn that they will not

notice the heroin.'

On each occasion that this man gave me such information I always passed it on.

A few weeks passed and, once again I found myself in deep conversation with him. 'See her Boss, 'the man indicated a female officer with a slight nod of his head.

'Yes, I can see her,' I replied. The lady in question was in her thirties, well-dressed, attractive, with a lovely figure. 'What about her?' I asked civilly.

The man gave an unpleasant leer. 'The other day Boss,' he whispered quietly.

'I was in the linen room when she walked in. I was standing on the chair stacking laundry and she unzipped my jeans and gave me a blow job.'

I gave an indifferent yawn as I unsuccessfully tried to convey my total and complete indifference, disbelief and boredom at these lies. 'What happened next?' I inquired casually.

'Well she swallowed it and then walked out of the room,' the unpleasant, dirty, smelly man commented. 'What do you think of that Boss?' he asked.

'Sounds good,' I commented casually. I did not believe one word of this

fantasy.

What should I have done?'

I should have spoken to the Wing Manger and informed him of this story.

Then I should have visited the Security Department and handed them an S.I.R.

report detailing every word he had told me.

What did I do?

Nothing.

This man was trying to score points with the staff to make himself look good. I

have no problem with that. It was just his slimy, unpleasant personality that I

disliked. Perhaps I am a bit old fashioned, but I cherish an abiding dislike of the sneak. In the prison service the grass is an essential part of the mechanisms to

make prisons run safely. But that does not mean that you like them. I did

believe that he fantasied about this pretty, prison officer. I did not believe one

word of his schoolboy fantasy. And I was not prepared to mark her file with

such an accusation just on the unsubstantiated word of an unpleasant, slimy

grass.

All police and prison staff make a clear distinction between the inmate who

perhaps informs on another con because he is genuinely disgusted with his

crimes and behaviour and the creep who comes crawling round staff simply in

order to curry favour.

The lady in question later told me that this inmate had been sternly admonished

by her, and by the Wing Manager, because of his habit of invading her personal

body space and making suggestive comments to her.

THE MURDERER.

A young lad entered my little office in Admissions and stood there facing me.

He was a scruffily dressed boy in his early twenties. He had the cocky, arrogant

air about him of someone who thinks he is important. 'Alright mate,' he

announced calmly. 'What happens now? Are you the Doctor?'

'I'm a psychiatric nurse,' I replied truthfully. I had a dozen A4 sized green,

wing files on the desk in front of me.
'What's your name?' I inquired politely.

The boy gave a smug, self-satisfied smile. 'You know who I am,' he boasted

proudly. 'Don't try it on with me. You know what I'm in for. Don't try and pull

the innocent act with me,' he gave another unpleasant smirk. 'Is this part of the

treatment?' he asked with another unpleasant leer. 'You pretend you don't know

who I am,' he gave another cynical grin.

It transpired that this lad had just been remanded for murder and he expected me

to be impressed.

I was not.

He seemed to think that this made him special in some way.

It did not.

He had never been in custody before.

It showed.

I gave a very weary and tired grin which was not difficult. 'I don't have the

faintest idea who you are or what you have been charged with.' I replied

truthfully.

'Not much you don't,' he replied with a triumphant grin. 'I bet you know my

whole, bloody life story by now.'

This is a very common behaviour pattern with some inmates. Many of them

assume that the staff spend their spare time poring over, 'the Files,' and

assimilating fascinating data about the inmates. They vaguely imagine huge

voluminous books or computers which detail every aspect of their lives from birth and school days onwards. And they honestly believe that the staff have

nothing better to do than to eagerly scan through all of this. The truth is much

more prosaic and much more boring. Most prison files contain the scantiest of

information anyway and in a dispersal jail such as Altcourse there could easily

be over a hundred admissions and an equal number of discharges in a week. No

one could conceivably keep track of such a vast turnover of inmates. And staff

quickly become bored and jaded when faced with an unending litany of new

inmates and each one of them believes his case is special.

'My mate is in here.' the boy boasted. 'He's a big gangster. He runs this place.

All of the screws are scared stiff of him.' The lad named his mate and, funnily enough I did know the man he was describing. This 'Big Gangster,' was a well-

known idiot and petty criminal. A man who made his own life inside as difficult

as possible and tried to make life as difficult as possible for other prisoners and

staff.

Most inmates have two very important priorities in jail. Their priority is to get

out as soon as possible. Their other priority is to make life as comfortable as

possible for themselves while inside. But there is always the idiot who makes

life difficult for everyone. The young lad seemed to think that I would gasp in

awe and give him special treatment when he told me he was best mates with

'Big Danny.'

It is difficult not to yawn when you listen to this claptrap hour after hour, day after day.

As I have already explained, in cases like this even if you are well acquainted

with the so-called, 'Big Gangster,' you always shrug and say. 'I've never heard

of him. 'I took about twenty minutes in completing a full mental, physical and

social assessment. This includes taking the blood pressure and pulse, recording

any injuries, illness, scars, operations mental illness, drug or alcohol problems

and any other matter of mental, social or physical interest.

Whenever a new admission charged with murder, manslaughter or attempted

murder was admitted to Altcourse Prison he would be placed on the Healthcare

Centre for observation. Many people first admitted to jail for serious crimes are initially suicidal and depressed and can attempt suicide or self-harm, but

experience has shown that within a few days most of them settle down and

come to terms with their situation. For these reasons they usually spend some

time in the Hospital Unit.

When I informed the lad of this fact, he was very annoyed. 'Look mate. I don't

want to go to the Hospital Wing,' he expostulated. 'I want to be with my pals.

What happens if I refuse to go there?'

The boy seemed to think that he could dictate his own terms. He also appeared

bored stiff by all of this and repeatedly asked, or rather told me when he could

go into the 'real prison' with his, 'Best Mate.'

'Don't be in such a hurry,' I chided. 'You are facing life imprisonment. You have got plenty of time.'

'So, what happens if I refuse to go the prison hospital?' he repeated.

I looked at him seriously. 'You are facing a life sentence in prison,' I repeated

seriously. 'I certainly would not advise you to start a long stretch by getting

nicked and twisted up.'

The very next day the boy was seen by the Doctor who read my assessment of

him and transferred the lad immediately to ordinary location.

ONE WEEK LATER.

I entered the wing and sat down in the dining area. This area is simply a large

part of the wing which is flanked by serving tables from which meals are

served. The chairs and tables are bolted to the floor and are plastic anyway, so they would not be of much use as weapons. The cutlery is also plastic. Metal

cutlery can be too easily be used or modified for use as weapons. I always

preferred to see men in the dining area. If they become upset or violent then

there are always prison officers on the Wing Console and, more importantly you

have a witness if there are any problems.

I sat and chatted to several men. They were all straightforward and I dealt with

them, one by one, as they were assigned to me by the officers. The young lad

who I have previously described was sitting quietly in one corner and he looked

desperately unhappy. In fact, he looked as if he was going to cry. The 'Big

Gangster,' who was his, 'Best Mate' was there playing snooker with a couple of other lads and as he wandered round the table crouching to take various shots at

the balls he constantly turned to the young lad and, each time he made a shot he

would shout, 'MURDERER,' at the top of his voice. Most of the prisoners

looked bored stiff. The officers approached the, 'Big Gangster' several times

and told him to shut up. Each time they did so he would politely agree, then,

seconds later, resume his behaviour.

I finished dealing with my last interview and was writing some notes. I was not

surprised when they young lad who I have previously described approached me.

'Can I speak to you please Doctor?" he asked tearfully.

'Sit down,' I requested and gestured to an empty chair. 'What can I do for

you?" I asked.

I made a mental guess as to what he was going to ask. I was right.

'I hate it on here,' he sobbed quietly. 'It's horrible. It's not like I thought it

would be. I want to go back to the Hospital Wing.'

I have seen this behaviour pattern a thousand times with various inmates

'You were admitted to the Hospital Unit because you were charged with

murder,' I explained patiently. 'You were there for assessment. You were

assessed. Both the doctor and I judged you fit for normal location. When you

were there you yourself told me that you wanted to be on ordinary location with

your 'Best Mate.' I gestured towards his 'friend' who was playing snooker.

'You got exactly what you asked for,' I explained. 'So, what are you complaining about?'

'Yes, I know,' he sobbed. 'But I hate it on here. Can't I be transferred back to

the hospital wing and serve my time there?'

'The hospital wing is for people who are ill. You are not ill,' I explained

reasonably.

'But I'm being bullied on here. I am under threat.'

If you are being bullied,' I explained. 'Then you have to go onto Reynoldstown

Blue which is a wing specially for the VPs.'

'But that is where the sex offenders are,' he protested.

I did not laugh. I did not ask. 'How are you getting on with Big Danny? You

know. Your best mate? The one who keeps on shouting out 'murderer?''

Instead I simply told him the truth.

'When you came in here,' I explained patiently. 'I told you that you were

looking at a life sentence and that is exactly what you are looking at. So, you

had better get used to it.'

As the Great Man said.

'Welcome to the real-world sonny boy.'

An interesting foot note to this story was an episode a few weeks later when I

was asked to attend a 'lift.' (A Lift is simply an episode when a con who is

known to be violent and difficult is transferred against his will to another area)

The 'Big Gangster,' was told that he had been, 'Adulted up.' In simple English

this means that although he was only nineteen, he would spend his days on the

Adult wing with men of twenty-one and over. But after bang-up he would be

marched across to the Young Prisoners Wing to sleep there. Young men like

'Big Danny,' are far less fearsome on Adult Wings. Older men are far better

equipped to deal with such boys.

THE JUNKIE.

Sometimes an inmate will ask for a detox simply because most drug users will

cheerfully abuse anything and everything and anything is better than nothing is

better than nothing. Occasionally though a lad comes along who states

emphatically. 'I don't want a detox. I am going to do my rattle. I am going to do

it cold and I am going to get off this muck.' With a man like that you shake his hand wish him luck and hope he succeeds. Sometimes though in many cases

there is a hidden agenda. One of the more laughable cases I came across was a

man, who informed me he wanted to come off methadone. This sounded like a

great idea.

When Dr No was the senior Doctor in Altcourse and he dealt with drug addicts

he had a very simple programme. He would prescribe a reducing regime of

DF118s over a two-week period which gradually reduced to nothing. (DF118s

are pain killers sometimes prescribed to help addicts cope with withdrawal.)

Numerous inmates protested at this, but the Doctor was adamant. In the first ten

years that I was there ONE inmate was given methadone. I don't know why he was special but for some reason he was. Not one man ever died from drug

withdrawal although thousands of them protested that they would. (They lied!)

In many prisons at the time methadone was legally prescribed by prison Doctors

but Dr No refused to do this. I personally cannot understand why governments

allow methadone to be prescribed anyway. It is simply another form of opiate

and the theory that drug addicts will be weaned off heroin and then come off

methadone is rubbish. I met people who have been on methadone for over

twenty years or even more. Not much sign of coming off drugs there.

At some point the situation changed. The government ordered that prison

Doctors must prescribe methadone.

This Doctor left Altcourse and a methadone regime started.

SOME TIME LATER.

A man approached me. He wanted to come off methadone. I made him a

Doctor's appointment and he repeated his request. He had been on eighty mils

of methadone daily for many years. The Doctor agreed that he could go onto a

reducing regime and suggested that he should reduce by five mils every day

until he was clean of drugs. This was a reasonable offer and for someone who

wanted to come off drugs, whether methadone or heroin it was a good idea.

The inmate was horrified.

The inmate suggested that he should reduce by, wait for it,

ONE HALF A MIL MONTHLY.

In simple terms he would be on 79 ½ mils daily rather than 80 mils.

When I heard this, I had to refrain from bursting out laughing.

The machine does not exist that can measure such miniscule amounts and the

idea that this is 'coming off drugs,' is laughable. It would be quite literally

impossible to measure the difference that such tiny doses of medication would

make to a person's physical and/or mental state.

As usual one of his 'friends,' told me the true story. The man was due in court

and wanted his brief to be able to say. 'My client is determined to get off drugs

My Lord. In fact, he has voluntarily entered a reducing regime and is

determined to break himself of this habit.'

When the man was informed of all of this, he, very generously volunteered to

come off his methadone at the rate of ONE MIL MONTHLY. Of course, once

the trial was over, he fully intended to report sick and change his mind and

demand his one mil back again. (Again, one of his friends told me this.)

The Doctor informed him that there was no point at all in reducing by such tiny

amounts. In court the inmate then protested that he had wanted to 'come off,'

methadone but the Doctor would not help him in any way. Apparently when the

prosecution barrister informed the court of the whole story the judge took a

rather jaundiced view of the whole matter.

THE PSYCHOPATH.

This boy was from a small town and even for Altcourse he was exceptional. He

was in his early twenties when I met him. Of a night he would beg, borrow,

burgle or steal money then go out and abuse as much alcohol and drugs as he

could. Like many such lads he got annoyed very easily. He would mix cocaine

with alcohol which is an incredibly potent and explosive mixture and then

physically assault anyone who annoyed him. If no-one annoyed him then he

would simply attack anyone he felt like attacking. He attacked people who

refused to lend him money, who refused to buy him alcohol, who refused to

give him credit. Sometimes he attacked people who he had never met before

because he did not like the way they looked at him. One time he asked some old man, for a cigarette and when the old chap replied. 'I don't smoke,' he attacked

him with a bar stool. It is a wonder that he never killed anyone. On different

occasions he physically attacked old men, and old women who were guilty, in

his eyes of something or other.

Not surprisingly he was extremely unpopular in his own town. On occasion

some of the local lads would team up, have a few beers and give him a good

kicking. Whenever this happened there were never any witness. For some

strange reason!

On numerous occasions his mother and father tried to get help from the local

psychiatric services. Several times he was admitted to various Mental Health

Units for treatment because someone, somewhere, believed that he had a mental illness and could be 'treated' and/or 'cured.'

Then whenever and wherever any nurse, doctor or any other professional tried

to enforce any kind of rules or regulations or indeed any kind of discipline

whatever on this dysfunctional young boy then the same, highly indignant

parents would scream from the rooftops that 'their boy,' was being abused.

A constant on-going problem with people like this is the fact that until they kill

someone it is next to impossible to get any realistic, mental treatment for them.

The high-security hospitals like Broadmoor and Ashworth are crammed to

overflowing with people who have killed and raped people in conditions of

extreme brutality. And just to add to the problem it seems that some of these hospitals want to keep inmates such as Ian Brady and Peter Sutcliffe because of

their notoriety. This simply adds to their overcrowding and makes such

admissions even more difficult.

When I met this lad, he explained to me that he was mentally ill, that he was not

responsible for his actions and that I (that is me personally) was responsible for

him being in custody.

He was sporting two glorious black eyes and when I met him, he told me that he

should immediately be transferred to a hospital because 'a right shower of

bastards,' in his hometown had attacked him.

I explained that he had seen a prison doctor that morning and his injuries were

superficial. He did not remotely need to go to a hospital.

It then transpired that he did not want to attend and A and E unit. No! He

wanted to be admitted to a Mental Health Unit for treatment for his so-called

'mental illness.'

He then gave me the names of the men who had attacked him. He wanted me to

phone the police and have them arrested. When I declined to complete 'this

'little job,' for him he was highly indignant.

'You are supposed to be on my side, you bastard,' he ground out through

clenched teeth. 'Those bastards beat me up. They could have killed me.'

'Why did they beat you up?' I asked.

'Well they said that I had attacked people,' he claimed.

'Is that true?' I asked.

He looked at me in utter and complete indignation. 'How the hell do I know?'

he asked indignantly. He gave a surprised snort. It was obvious that he neither

knew nor cared who he had had beaten up and who he had attacked. 'You don't

seem to understand,' he shouted. 'I am mentally ill. My psychiatrist told me that

I had an emotionally deprived childhood. I am not responsible for my actions. It

is up to you to get me out of this shithole and get me released.'

'If you want people prosecuted then you should go to the police,' I suggested.

I made myself keep a straight face as I made this suggestion.

'I did,' he shouted.

'Well what happened?' I asked.

'They laughed at me,' he complained bitterly. 'One copper told me that I needed a few good hidings.'

He rambled on at me and stated emphatically that when in this jail he wanted

prison officers sacked because they 'treated him like a criminal,' and had

'beaten him up.' By this he meant that he had been twisted up on a couple of

occasions when he had threatened or assaulted other inmates or staff.

At one point he said to me. 'You give the impression that you couldn't give a

fuck about me.'

I was tempted to say to laugh in his face and say. 'A flash of intelligence.' I

didn't!'

This boy requested or rather, absolutely demanded, that I should issue his local

Police Force with instructions that he had a personality disorder (on that one issue he was right) and that when arrested he should immediately be released without charge. He further demanded that Altcourse Jail should instruct a psychiatrist to issue an order to make it impossible for any police officer anywhere to arrest him ever for any offence at all. He also wanted our psychiatrist to give him a letter which he could carry around with him and which instructed any police officer that he must not be arrested under any circumstances.

He didn't want much did he?

It is amazing to recount a story like this, but readers will be interested that although he was an extreme case there are literally thousands of people like him in and out of jail.

When you spent a lifetime, as I did, working with these people then you are

extremely grateful that prison exists. It is the only place where such dangerous

nut cases can be incarcerated safely and where they can be kept away from

normal human beings. The sad thing is when you meet some kind-hearted, well-

meaning, do-gooder who lectures you at length all about how you should show

care and compassion to such people because they are mentally ill and should be

treated with respect. It is also interesting when such people personally encounter

psychopaths and either they themselves or their families or friends are burgled,

assaulted, raped and/or otherwise molested in some way. Invariably when such

an episode happens then the 'do-gooder,' instantly becomes overnight one of the 'hang them and flog them' brigade.

The Mental Health Act definition of a psychopath is a person who has 'a

persistent disorder or disability of mind which results in abnormally aggressive

or seriously irresponsible behaviour and is not amenable to reason.' This lad

certainly, seemed to fit this bill of goods perfectly.

The fact is that psychopaths like this are not in the slightest bit mentally ill.

And, of course they are completely responsible for their own actions.

People who want respect should give respect.

THE BANKER.

This was another of my many acquaintances during my years inside.

He was a middle-aged man who had worked in a large, prestigious bank and at

some point, he got sticky fingers. He embezzled a huge sum of money. When

the fraud was discovered he was arrested and at some point, he was offered a

plea bargain.' He was promised by 'someone,' that if he gave the money back,

he would be let off with three years. With remission he would be out in just

over a year. But! If he did not return the cash, then he would get five years. The

man thought it over and decided to take the five years.

'After all,' he explained to me. 'No bank in the world will ever employ me

again. I might as well keep the bloody money. And do the time.' The other

inmates were well impressed with him particularly because he decided to do the extra time and kept the money. This all fits the myth of the victimless crime in

which 'no one suffers.' This is rubbish. No one dispute that big banks and other

multi-national companies are worse criminals than ordinary thieves. But the

banks always offload their losses onto the public so in the end we all pay for his

crime. Big banks certainly do not make any kind of loss due to money which is

stolen off them.

The accountant explained to me that he had the cash safe in a tax haven in the

West Indies. Apparently, his mistress was there to keep an eye on his

investment. 'What are you going to do if she meets a new boyfriend and loses

interest in you or spends the lot while you are inside?' I asked curiously.

He grinned. 'She can only touch the interest,' he explained.

I had already decided to SIR these facts, but I did say. 'I am surprised you are

telling me this.'

He laughed. 'No one can touch my money.' He then named the island in

question and told me. 'That place is an independent country and it lives off

illicit money.' He grinned. 'And postage stamps and tourism,' he added. 'When

I get out I will go and live there. I used to love going sailing and fishing in the

Caribbean,' and again the man gave a wide grin and I guessed that he was

dreaming of blue skies, bikini-clad beauties on golden sands and sailing across

azure seas in a fishing boat.

One little detail seemed to escape his notice and the notice of his fellow crooks.

It was not HIS cash. It belonged to the British public.

There is no such thing as a victimless crime.

THE STUDENT.

One day I walked onto a Wing accompanied by a young student. He seemed a

cheerful and chatty lad and asked all sorts of questions. In those days I used to

do a lot of clay pigeon shooting and I had taken various members of staff

shooting with me. He asked me all sorts of questions about guns and shooting.

He wanted to know how to obtain a gun licence and all about what kind of

security was needed. He even asked me all about my own collections of

firearms and all about my own security. I had no reason to be reticent, so I answered freely. I assumed that, like many young men he was just interested in

shooting. When we visited one wing, he drifted over to an officer who was

standing next to the Information Board and the two of them spent some time

chatting. This Board is simply a huge panel which lists all the prisoners on that

wing along with the briefest of information. It usually details the inmate's

status sentenced or remanded, their date of birth and other brief data. I was

talking to a second officer while they were chatting.

The next day when I went into work the student was not there. To be honest I

never even gave him another thought. I was too busy.

A few days later I visited that same Wing and the prison officer who had conversed with the student approached me. 'I'm really sorry about that Chris,'

he explained profusely. 'I had to do that. I had no choice.'

'What on earth are you talking about?' I asked.

I had no idea what he was referring to.

It transpired that this student had been asking all sorts of very detailed questions

all about the security of one inmate including the details of when he next visited

court and the timings of prison wagons. And, for good measure the inmate was

a Cat 'A' prisoner accused of serious crimes involving firearms and violence.

When he tried to enter the prison the next day the Student was interrogated by

the Security Department and it transpired that he had close connections to this

inmate.

The Officer whom the student had been trying to pump for information had, quite rightly, completed an SIR (Security Information Report) and handed it in.

I never saw that student again. Apparently, his security clearance was withdrawn. He was not sacked. He just could not work there anymore. A very nice distinction.

One of the girls asked me. 'What are you going to do if he contacts you and asks you to take him shooting?"

I am not given to swearing but every so often ordinary English is simply not expressive enough.

'There are two very good words of English for such a request,' I explained succinctly. 'The second one of which is OFF.'

I never saw or heard from that student again ever.

THE ACTOR.

In Admissions one night and a colleague gave some young lad a DF118 tablet.

DF118 is a mild pain killer issued to people for pain. It is also given in cases of

drug withdrawal for the supposed signs and symptoms of withdrawal. Every

young lad claims to be withdrawing from drugs or to be mentally ill or to need

tranquilisers, or pain killers or sleeping tablets. It is truly amazing just how

badly the GPs in the Community prescribe drugs totally inappropriately to

anyone and everyone.

Another young lad approached me. 'You refused to give me any tablets,' he shouted indignantly. 'But my mate here was given something by that other

nurse. Why is that?'

I shrugged indifferently.

'Obviously, he is a better actor than you,' I explained.

THE ARTIST.

On occasion while carrying out my usual routine in Altcourse Jail I visited a

particular lad in his cell. He was a tall, well-built, broad-shouldered, young boy,

handsome in a rather battered way. He was talkative but, like many of these

boys, his speech was laced with four letter words. Quite literally almost every

other word he uttered was 'fuck. This is common behaviour with these lads.

We got chatting and, to my surprise he started asking me about myself which is

highly unusual. In jail most of the inmates simply want to talk about

themselves. This a bonus for Mental Health Nurses as it makes it easier to

obtain information. He chatted away about himself, his crimes, his drinking,

drug taking and his womanising. He also seemed genuinely interested both in

myself and my own background. He asked how I had got into the job, what it

entailed and what the training was like? These questions were unusual.

Sometimes when an inmate is asking you questions you must be careful. He

may well have a hidden agenda. Not necessarily for himself but possibly for one

of his friends who has taken a dislike to you. For some reason! Any reason! No reason! He could be seeking information about which area you live in, which

public houses you drink in or any other information that might enable someone

to track you down. Fortunately, inmates are very changeable in their priorities.

This week you may well be top of the hate list and, if by chance you ran into

such a lad outside and he is carrying a weapon then there could be trouble. But

usually in a week's time he has found someone else to hate. To be fair this boy

did not appear threatening to me in any way. In fact, he was cheerful,

loquacious and friendly.

There was an A4 folder in his cell which, by chance, was laying half-open. The

first page was a well-drawn picture. It was an illustration of a masked gunman robbing a security wagon. I asked permission to look through his folder and was

impressed with his obvious talent. I have no knowledge of art, but it was clear

that his skill was first-class. And every single one of his pictures depicted crime

and violence. We continued chatting and we built up a good rapport.

One of the things that came across very strongly was that he considered himself

a criminal and had no interest in any other possible career. All his friends and

acquaintances were crooks and he talked constantly about crime. I went back

several times to visit him. He did seem to listen to and to respond to my advice.

It was the fourth, possibly my fifth visit, but anyway it was the last. I sat in his cell and considered him for one moment. Sometimes when you are working in a

job like mine you experience a feeling of despair. You are being paid money to

do a job. You put your enthusiasm and your energy into it for years on end. But

every so often you really feel that you have reached a dead end. Here was a boy

with a great deal of talent. No! Not talent. Genius! And his ambition was to be a

big-time drug-dealer.

There are many old jokes in psychiatry.

One very old joke is this.

Question. 'What is it that every-one gives? And no-one takes?'

Answer. 'Advice.'

There is nothing more annoying than when a person asks for your advice and you spend time and trouble in giving them truthful and positive advice and the

person either completely ignores you, or alternatively gets angry when you give

them the answer they do not want.

Also, many psychiatric nurses find it very annoying when people expect you to

listen to them, but they will not listen to you.

But this boy was unusual. He not only listened, he was genuinely interested in

my replies. And, just as a side issue, I have to say, that I enjoyed his company.

He was quite witty, obviously intelligent, and within his limited experiences he

was knowledgeable and talkative.

In the prison service staff quickly become very cynical. I never had that

problem. I was very cynical anyway.

One day we sat and chatted together. I considered him thoughtfully before I

spoke. For a moment I wondered if I should just shrug my shoulders and walk

away. No one would ever know. I doubt if anyone would even care. But I made

a decision. I decided to attempt to do the job I was paid to do.

'When you get out of jail,' I suggested slowly. 'Instead of selling drugs have

you ever considered enrolling in Art School and taking up art as a career?'

He looked at me calmly and seriously. 'It's funny you should say that Boss,' he

commented slowly. 'In my last jail there was a screw who used to come and talk

to me. Just like you. And he was always talking to me about me studying art.'

The lad paused thoughtfully for a moment before he spoke. 'He was sound for a screw,' the boy stated slowly. 'But a right cunt like me would stand no fucking

chance in Art School Boss.' He shrugged philosophically. 'It would be full of

posh bastards and stuck-up bitches and when they found out I'd been in jail

they'd fuck me off.'

I explained to this lad that plenty of working-class boys and girls attend colleges

of all kinds and that many of them succeed and qualify in various subjects. I

went on to explain that if he did well at art and passed a degree then all sorts of

positions would be open to him. Unfortunately, I myself, know little or nothing

about art as a possible career. Nevertheless, I advised him to visit his local job

centre and inquire there. I knew that they would be able to give him information on possible careers. There could be positions in architecture, design, and

advertising. I went on to explain that some of the 'posh bastards' in Art College

would be pretty girls and that some of them would fancy him.

He was further amazed. 'Posh birds fancy me Boss?' he expostulated. 'You

must be fucking joking. All the birds I've shagged have all been right, fucking

slags.'

'No. I am not joking,' I explained. 'But, incidentally, if you want to date a nice

girl then your chances will be far better if you stop swearing.'

He looked at me for one long moment in genuine curiosity. 'What difference

will that make?' I explained that many girls are sensitive about obscene language and if he was courting a girl then she would be embarrassed if she

took him to meet her friends and relatives and he continually used foul speech. I

watched his face as he listened to me and slowly nodded.

'Great!' I thought! 'I have actually got through to him.'

Some days later I went to visit this lad and it transpired that he had been

shipped. (SHIPPED; sent to another jail.)

I often wonder what became of this boy. I sincerely hope that he attended

college, passed a First-Class degree in art, got a good job, met a nice girl,

married her and retired from crime.

But I expect he is either dead or sitting in a Maximum-Security Jail somewhere

serving life for murder, drugs and armed robbery.

Still! I did my best.

THE VEGETARIAN.

On occasion I admitted two new men. Both were committed supporters of

animal rights. They had just received five years each for burning butchers

shops. Neither of them had ever been in jail before.

The first man was cheerful and chatty. He showed no remorse or sorrow over

what they had done. On the contrary he appeared quite proud of his actions. 'At

least they have not killed or injured anyone,' I thought philosophically to

myself.

I gave him the usual spiel about how to behave, what to do and, more importantly what not to do. He appeared surprised at my attitude to him.

'You seem sympathetic towards us,' he explained.

'Look at it from my point of view,' I answered. 'I meet child murderers,

rapists, terrorists. You are just two more new inmates.'

He looked at me closely. 'Will we get picked on and attacked by staff and

prisoners because of our beliefs?" he inquired seriously.

'I very much doubt it,' I replied truthfully. 'As a matter of fact, many prisoners

respect someone who is in jail for strongly held beliefs rather than for just

theft and violence,' I paused. 'And, not that it will make it any easier for you,

but I personally, agree with a lot of the, 'Green Party,' beliefs. I am one hundred per cent in favour of saving protected and endangered species of animals. I

think that the way in which governments the world over are polluting and

destroying the countryside, the environment and the oceans with plastics and

rubbish is disgusting. I totally support using less, fossil fuels and trying to get

this world back onto a more sensible ecological road. I believe that the answer

to these problems is massive birth control which will reduce the world

population so that we could have a sustainable population without doing

irreparable harm to the environment.'

The man looked at me in amazement. 'That is amazing,' he stated flatly. 'I

never thought I would hear a prison officer talk like that,' he paused and regarded me curiously. 'Are you a vegetarian?' he asked.

I kept it non-committal. I just shrugged and replied. 'No, I am not a veggie. As a

matter of fact, I love eating meat. And incidentally. I am not a prison officer. I

am a psychiatric nurse.'

'Eating meat is not just murder,' he explained. 'It does not make any kind of

ecological sense. The amount of land required to produce one cow which is then

murdered for meat could produce far more grain and vegetables far more

economically.'

I shrugged. 'It's a very complex issue. Unfortunately, I have not got the time

to discuss it all with you. We agree on many issues and disagree on others.'

'But you seem to understand our cause,' he protested. 'Despite the fact that you like eating dead bodies.' He then asked me he could go about getting vegetarian

meals while in jail.

I laughed out loud. He seemed to think that this would be a big issue.

In the famous prison movie Scum one of the heroes is a vegetarian who refuses

to eat meat and insists on going barefoot because he will not wear leather boots.

He also describes himself as an atheist so each Sunday he must be supervised by

a prison officer while everyone else attends chapel.

What a load of old rubbish!

In real life of course, no one would give two hoots if this silly boy chose to go

barefoot while inside. No one would suffer except himself. And, nowadays all

you do to get a special diet is to tick the box on the form which is given to every new inmate on admission.

And why on earth would a prison officer be detailed to supervise this idiot. The

lad would just be left to sit all alone in a cell with his own, silly, little self while

the other lads would be free to visit chapel, get out to of their cells for a couple

of hours, break the day up and have a chance to meet their friends and have a

friendly chat.

I explained all of this to my new-found friend. He thanked me, I wished him all

the best and we shook hands.

The second admission that day was the co-accused of my previous admission.

He was a totally different proposition from the first, happy, chatty arsonist. The

second man was close-mouthed and taciturn. He responded to the simplest of my questions with suspicion and distrust. He point-blank refused to answer

various questions on the admissions form. He seemed to think that this would

annoy me or cause me trouble. This does not happen. We simply write down.

'Refused to answer!' No-one cares.

'It is people like you who keep the rich capitalists in power,' he accused me. He

was very angry. 'You are a stooge of the fascists,' he informed me. 'There is a

war on between the neo-Nazi governments and working-class people. And you

are a war criminal. You are an Imperialist running dog, a capitalist hyena, a

fascist lackey. You have sold out your principles to become a wage slave of the

Capitalist State.' He certainly knew all the jargon off by heart.

People like this always bring out the worst in me. I could not help but grin. 'No!

You are wrong,' I protested vehemently. 'I never sold out my principles. You

see I never had any principles in the first place. So, I couldn't sell them out.'

I suppose I shouldn't really have fallen into the trap but when you meet

someone like this it is difficult to take such pompous, self-opinionated people

seriously.

'You disgust me,' the man grated out through clenched teeth.

Just like all fanatics he had no sense of humour.

I really couldn't have cared less.

THE IDIOT.

A young man came into the prison. He told me that he had assaulted a female

nurse in a Casualty Unit. Apparently, he attended this unit on an extremely,

hectic day and was eventually interviewed by this busy lady. His problem was

that he did not have a girlfriend and he felt that the NHS should do something

about this matter.

In every crowded and overworked Accident and Emergency Unit the nurses,

Doctors and other staff are frequently confronted with heart attacks, strokes,

epileptic fits and injuries from Road Traffic Accidents. People come in with

wounds from guns, knives, broken bottles and iron bars. A member of staff may

watch someone die and do their best to console their husband or wife and, then minutes later, be expected to attend a bad-tempered person who demands instant

attention for a cut finger. There is also an endless litany of complaints from

people who have totally unrealistic demands and expectations. I once witnessed

a man attend an A and E unit at four 'o' clock in the morning with a bad back

which he had suffered for the last three years. When the Doctor asked him why

he had left it so long to seek treatment he replied. 'Well I've just been for a

couple of beers and I thought I'd pop in for some treatment.' I have personally

witnessed people who dialled 999 because they are constipated or had a pimple

on the chin.

I was brought up to be proud of the British Health Service as an outstanding institution but when you encounter idiots like this you cannot help but wonder it

the American system should be adopted.

I have to say though that, on balance, I am glad and proud of the NHS and

personally, I would never swap it for the American system.

When the Accident and Emergency nurse explained to this lad that she was

exceptionally busy and that he was making totally unrealistic demands he

physically attacked her and injured her. He ended up in jail and he was very

annoyed about this.

This boy who wanted a girlfriend explained to me that if not having a girlfriend

made him so depressed and upset then the Health Service had a legal and moral

duty to help him with this problem. I was a psychiatric nurse, so it was my responsibility to get him out of jail and furthermore to find him a girlfriend.

'You are wrong,' I explained. 'It is your own job to find yourself a girlfriend.

Try joining social clubs. Take up a hobby like dancing where you will meet lots

of females. Join a dating agency. But all of that is up to you. And incidentally it

is not my job to get you out of jail. When you go to court try apologising to the

lady you attacked, speak politely to the judge and say that you are sorry and will

accept any punishment he gives you.'

The lad was highly indignant. 'You can't talk to me like that,' he protested

vehemently. 'You are supposed to care for me. I am a mentally ill boy and you

are in a position of trust. You cannot avoid your responsibilities in this way.'

'Who told you all of this?' I inquired in genuine curiosity.

'My social worker,' he replied.

I didn't even bother arguing with this.

Instead I simply spoke to him clearly and concisely. 'Listen to me,' I ordered.

'It is your own responsibility to find yourself a girlfriend. But remember this! If

you even touch one of the females in here you will find yourself in big trouble.

For a start you will be twisted up and sent to the Block. Then after that you will

be charged with assault.'

'You are not allowed to threaten me,' the lad protested indignantly. He stared

straight at him and I gave him back stare for stare.

'I am not threatening you,' I stated flatly. 'I am promising you exactly what will happen to you if you assault any female staff member in here.'

The boy started crying. This is a behaviour pattern which he had obviously

learnt on the out. It normally works outside of jail. It seldom works inside.

Never once, in all my years inside, did, I ever lose my temper although

sometimes I came very close. That day I came extremely close. 'Listen to me,

you idiot,' I explained lucidly. 'You are not mentally ill. You are unhappy.

Unhappiness is not a mental illness. Not having a girlfriend is not a mental

illness either.' The boy now looked even unhappy. 'Welcome to the real-world

sonny boy,' I informed him.

THE DINOSAUR.

Newbold Revel is an 18th-century country house in the village of Stretton-under

Foss in Warwickshire. It is now used by the Prison Service as a training base.

The old manor House is a Grade Two listed building. It was built in 1716 for Sir

Fulwar Skipwith. The estate was variously owned by wealthy individuals and

eventually by the Seventh Day Adventists. After the Second World War it

became a Catholic Training College and was sold again in 1978 to British

Telecom. In 1985 it was taken over by the Prison Service for its current use as

the Prison Service College.

My line manager told me that I had to attend a training course there. My

speciality in Altcourse Jail was always Admissions. This course was

particularly about Prison Admissions.

When I arrived there, we passed through security and checked in. The whole

estate was a huge, well cultivated area that must have covered many acres. It

contained many different buildings with many different purposes. The most

interesting one was a museum of Jail relics, souvenirs and artefacts which dated

back over the centuries.

I was really pleased to take this course and I found it fascinating. The training

staff were all friendly and knowledgeable.

We covered many different matters including admission and we did, 'role

plays,' in which we took on various staff positions. Afterwards there would be a

discussion on were the staff went wrong or did well.

I carried out one role play where I was an over-worked, tired, harassed

Admissions Nurse faced with an extremely unpleasant new admission who

shouted and swore at me and repeatedly refused my instructions. It was all great

fun. I was ordered to be particularly unpleasant in return. 'I was beaten up

by the fucking coppers,' he snarled at me, 'they battered me with their

truncheons. I want medication for my headaches.'

'Good!' I snarled indifferently in return. 'Give me their names and I'll drive up

there tonight and buy them a few pints.'

The point was made to the watching staff that the bad-tempered and tired nurse

totally missed the issue that the new patient might be brain damaged. The first

thing the nurse should have done was a thorough examination of the new man's head checking for boggy haematoma. (Boggy haematoma; an area of soft tissue

on the head after a head injury has been sustained) Also check for any possible

bleeding from the nose, mouth or ears. Next an examination of the man's eyes.

If the pupils are correct and react to light, then PEARL can be recorded.

(P.E.A.R.L. Pupils equal and reacting to light.) The nurse or doctor should also

check and record the person's orientation for time and place.

One day during this training I found myself sitting chatting with a lady

Psychiatrist. She was intelligent, knowledgeable, informative and easy to talk

to. We chatted freely and at one point she sat and regarded me calmly. 'Are you

a Prison Officer or a nurse?' she asked me.

'I am a nurse,' I explained. 'Why do you ask?'

'Are you a trained nurse? Or a Care Assistant?'

'As a matter of fact,' I replied. 'I am an R.M.N. and R.G.N.'

'You do not come across as a nurse,' she complained. 'You come across far

more strongly as a Prison Officer rather than as a nurse.'

I looked straight at her and gave her my friendly smile. 'Well we all have to do

the best we can,' I grinned.

She looked at me again and shook her head sadly. 'You are not a nurse,' she

expostulated. 'You are a Dinosaur.'

THE NEXT DAY.

I thought about the impression I had made on this lady and the next day I approached her. 'I've been thinking about what you said,' I explained seriously.

'You are wrong.'

She looked at me. 'Why am I wrong?' she asked warily.

'The dinosaurs became extinct because they could not adopt to a changing

environment,' I explained. 'I am here on this training course to learn how to

adopt to a changing environment. Therefore! Obviously! I cannot be a

dinosaur.'

To give the lady her due she sat and listened to me. Then she smiled as well.

'Alright,' she conceded. 'You are an intelligent dinosaur.'

THE OVERDOSE.

This lad claimed he had taken an overdose of pills, so the doctor referred him to

me for a psychiatric opinion. At first, we sat and chatted rationally. Then he

gave an exasperated sigh. 'These bleeding women Boss,' he complained

bitterly. 'They are more trouble than they are worth. It's all their fault that I

took an overdose. But when I saw the doctor, he would not help me in anyway.

Women are bloody nuisances. I don't know why men bother with them.

Bleeding women.'

I was tempted to reply. 'I don't know why women bother with men either.'

But I didn't.

Instead I asked curiously. 'What exactly do you call help?'

'Well some treatment. You know tablets.'

I gave an audible sigh. 'The treatment for an overdose of tablets is not more tablets,' I informed him patiently.

'Well what is it then?" he asked indignantly.

'Usually just time,' I explained. 'Or a hospital admission for a stomach wash out.'

'But I got nothing mate. Absolutely nothing.'

'What overdose did you take?' I asked curiously.

The lad thought for a moment and then spoke. 'I don't what they are called,' he stated. 'They belonged to my girlfriend. I pinched them off her and swallowed the entire contents of the bottle. I thought I might get high on them.' He grinned. 'Or low! I mean who bleeding cares so long as you get some kind of buzz.'

'When was this?' I asked.

Again, the lad seemed to be trying to think and this unusual feat was obviously

painful. Finally, he spoke. 'About a week ago,' he answered finally.

I laughed out loud. 'Well if you took these tablets a week ago then you are not

going to be harmed by them, now are you?' I pointed out.

'Yeah! But look mate. I want treatment. Proper treatment.'

'What do you call proper treatment?' I repeated.

'Valium or methadone,' he shouted angrily.

I was on the verge of just walking away when for some reason I decided to ask

him one last question. 'Tell me,' I requested. 'What exactly where these tablets that you stole off your girlfriend?'

Again, the lad thought deeply. 'Well it was like this see. You know what these

bleeding women are like Boss. She was having trouble with her periods and

these were tablets to make her start menstruating.'

I almost burst out laughing. It is a bad habit of mine.

'What will happen to me Boss?' the asked anxiously.

I was tempted to say. 'You will bleed to death.'

I didn't.

THE TRAMP.

When a man is admitted to jail the very first thing that the other inmates want to know is. 'What is he in for?' In a closed community there are no secrets and

inmates are always interested in any gossip.

I admitted an old man who looked as if he were in his seventies. He was

wearing a pair of army boots and about four overcoats. He himself and his

clothing was dirty, dishevelled and smelly. He had long straggly grey hair and

looked and smelt as if he had not washed or shaved for months. 'Hello Boss,' he

greeted me in a cheerful and friendly manner. 'Nice to meet you! How are you?

When will I get a cup of tea?'

I could not help but grin back. 'Nice to meet you,' I replied. 'What are you in

jail for?'

The man grinned again. 'Smashing widows Boss,' he announced cheerfully.

I looked carefully at the old guy. 'Been in jail before?' I asked.

The man grinned again. 'Lots of times Boss,' he answered politely.

'What exactly happened?' I inquired.

'I was a patient in a big, psychiatric hospital,' he explained. 'I was in there for

years. But the government closed them all down and kicked us all out. I did all

right. I touched lucky. I got put into a Nursing Home. It was alright there. I

quite liked it. I had a room to myself and everything was great. A lot of my

mates had been in those Big Bins for over fifty years. They can't cope with life

on the outside. Some of them can't even understand decimal cash. And a lot of

them need to be reminded to take their tablets regularly. So, when they miss their medication they go mad. A lot of them are dead. They freeze to death.

They commit suicide. They take drugs and die of an overdose,' the old man

gave a philosophical shrug. 'Some of them just die of loneliness and despair,'

he explained sadly.

When you meet some harmless old man like this who is walking the streets in a

British winter you cannot really blame him for actions like this. Mrs Thatcher in

her wisdom, closed the big mental hospitals back in the 1980's and 1990's in

order to save money. That is why people like me were paid a great deal of

money to look after the harmless derelicts of society who are admitted to the

one remaining institution which will give them a warm bed and food. Then the government point at the savings they claim to have made in the Health service

and boast that they are saving money. They do not explain about the huge cost

of keeping such people in jail. This is only one reason why Britain has more

people in jail per capita than other European country.

'How did you end up in here?' I asked quietly.

'One of the residents was a right swine. He was always stealing other people's

gear. One day I caught him robbing my room. I belted him one and hurt him

badly. The Manager told me off. She was alright. But, that day a social

worker came in to visit the thieving sod. She called the police and told him

to press charges. I got stuck in jail. By the time I was released I had lost my protected rights as a Nursing Home resident. I found myself walking the

streets.' He grimaced. 'It's bloody cold in winter Boss,' he explained.

'Exactly what happened?' I inquired.

The man grinned again. 'It's winter Boss,' he explained. 'And the weather

outside is freezing. And it is going to get colder before it gets warmer. I was

walking the streets and I'd had nothing to eat for three days. I smashed a shop

window and grabbed some pork pies and scoffed them,' he grinned again. 'I

like pork pies,' he explained. 'The police took ages to get there so I sat down

and scoffed the pies and then a couple of nice meat pasties,' the old man licked

his lips. 'They were delicious,' he boasted. 'When the cops finally did arrive, I put up a bit of a fight. I was hoping they would charge me with resisting arrest

or assaulting the police as well so that I would get longer in jail. I spent the

night in the cells and the cops were nice to me. I got a good meal and a cup of

tea.' Again, the old chap gave a good-humoured grin. 'But they just charged me

with theft and damage. The cops asked me if I wanted a lawyer, but I said I

would defend myself. I knew that the charges were enough to get me a jail

sentence. When I went up in front of the Magistrate, they read out my previous

convictions and the Bench were really annoyed with me. So, I told them all to

fuck off and they got even more annoyed with me,' the old man laughed out

loud.

You look at an old guy like this and say to yourself. 'There but for the Grace of

God.'

'How long did you get?' I inquired politely.

'Six months,' the old man boasted. 'Even with full remission I will get over the

worst of the winter weather.'

I honestly could not find it in my heart to blame him. I filled in the paperwork

and, to my amazement I discovered that he was twenty years younger me.

Mind you! He'd had a hard life.

'Behave yourself and you will I have no trouble here,' I promised him.

LATER.

On admission to jail you are given a burn pack which contains half an ounce of tobacco. Many inmates will have sweet pack instead. I watched the old man as

he sat with a group of inmates and with the dexterity of long practice rolled

himself a cigarette and inhaled greedily. The trusties were dishing out supper

and the old tramp gratefully scoffed his food and accepted an extra helping.

One of the trusties approached me. 'Tell me something Boss?' the man asked.

'That new fellah. Is he a nonce?' Staff are not supposed to discuss inmates with

other inmates but there is a stereotype of the nonce. He is regarded as a dirty,

old man.' My new admission certainly was dirty. He certainly was old. But he

certainly, was not a nonce.'

I looked straight at the trusty. 'He is not a nonce, 'I stated flatly. 'My word on

it.'

The man shrugged. 'Alright Boss,' he agreed. 'I believe you.'

Ten minutes later I heard a disturbance outside of my office door. I stuck my head out.

In one corner a group of very big men were sitting together eating their meal and chatting quietly to each other. They were all Cat 'A' prisoners on remand for murder. They were all members of a large, powerful gang and were accused of killing another gang member in conditions of extreme brutality. Most such men never cause staff the least trouble. The only time they are dangerous is if you impede an attempted escape. Then, if you get in their way, they will kill you. To men like this jail is simply an occupational hazard and they simply want to serve their time, make life as comfortable as possible for themselves

inside and get out as soon as possible.

A couple of very scared looking YPS (Young Prisoners) were being confronted

by two of these much older men.

I soon heard the story. Apparently, these obnoxious little boys confronted the

old man. They both squared up him, threatened him and, with no proof

whatever accused him of molesting children. For obvious reasons nonces are

unpopular with inmates.

When the two well-built, middle-aged convicts intervened and told the little

boys to behave themselves then, suddenly the two little boys were all sweetness

and light.

What a surprise!

THE BIG FELLAH!

A new admission to jail!

This man barged straight into my office without knocking, helped himself to a

chair and sat down. He sat there glaring straight at me. He appeared to be in a

bad mood. This is not unusual with prison admissions. Lots of them are in a bad

mood. But this man was exceptional. He was a big, tall, well-built, muscular,

unshaven man, roughly dressed in cheap, badly cared for clothes and a flashy

watch. He had about him the air of a man who thinks, or rather knows, that the

world was created especially for his benefit. He related the story about how he

had ended up in jail. Prisoners often want to tell their tale. This is harmless therapy and it does the prisoner good to get it off his chest. This man had been

convicted of Grievous Bodily Harm. One evening he was with 'HIS' woman.

(Funnily enough I thought that slavery had been abolished and no-one owned

anyone anymore. But perhaps this was too politically correct for him.)

Apparently, the lady was a very, well-endowed girl with big breasts and

backside. He ordered her to wear sexy underwear along with low-cut blouses or

tops and short dresses or skirts so that she could display her ample charms.

Nothing wrong with that most men would say. Sounds great in fact! One night

in a pub a drunk walked up to 'HIS' woman and felt her backside. No one

would condone this behaviour in any way! But I personally thought that deep down, he was quite pleased. He struck me as being the sort of man who went

around the world looking for someone to offend him so that he could get angry

and prove how tough he was. 'Everyone calls me, 'the Big Fellah,' he boasted.

'I can take anyone!' So naturally 'the Big Fellah,' stalked up to this unfortunate

drunk. 'You touch that cow again and I will kill you,' he warned. The drunk

didn't seem to take matters too seriously. He just grinned and made some inane

comment. The Big Fellah punched the drunk in the face and the man went

flying into a brick wall. He sustained a head injury and nearly died.

'Normally I would have just denied the whole thing,' the big man snarled

nastily. 'I always do. But the bar had a closed-circuit television and I was on film. And the landlord grassed me up and gave my name to the police. Bastard!'

He was given a custodial sentence. 'And my brief let me down,' the man

snarled nastily. 'He's another useless bastard.'

I was curious. 'What did your brief do wrong?' I inquired.

It was none of my business. I was just being nosey.

The man controlled his temper with an obvious effort then spoke. 'I have known

this lawyer for years,' he explained. 'Normally when I get arrested, he gets me

not guilty, or a fine, or community service or some shit like that but this time

the bloody judge wouldn't listen to anything that either of us said. Bloody

swine! So here I am in jail.'

'You could have killed the man,' I pointed out mildly.

'So, what,' he snarled. He seemed incapable of speaking without snarling. 'That

cow belongs to me,' he stated grimly. 'He had no right to touch it.'

(I loved the way he referred to the lady in question as 'THAT COW' and 'IT,'

And people criticise ME for being not being politically correct!)

'Do you lose your temper easily?' I inquired seriously.

'I can't control my temper,' he stated flatly. 'I've tried. But I can't. It's not my

fault. It's just the way I'm made. There's nothing I can do about it. Anyway, I

couldn't care less.'

'You have just been sentenced to three years in jail because of your bad temper,' I pointed out mildly. 'I take it that you couldn't care less about that either.'

He glared nastily at me. 'Don't be bloody stupid mate,' he snarled.

'If you behave yourself will be out in eighteen months,' I explained. 'And don't call me Mate.'

'Exactly does that mean?' he snarled. He seemed incapable of speaking without snarling.

I could not help myself. Every so often you meet someone who is so obnoxious that you simply must tell them the truth. 'It means that my name is not Mate,' I replied politely.

'What is your name then?' he asked nastily.

'Boss,' I answered flatly.

He looked at me in surprise. 'Boss?' he repeated.

'That's right,' I replied. 'You're beginning to learn.'

When I meet unpleasant people, I always feel that if they are making the effort

to be so unpleasant then I should oblige by making just as big an effort and

being unpleasant in return.

'Listen mate do you expect me to call you, Boss?' he asked incredulously.

'No! You listen to me,' I explained patiently. 'If you behave yourself then you

will get fifty percent remission. That means you will be out in eighteen months.

And, so long as you control your temper you will probably be transferred to an

open prison for the latter part of your sentence. Open prisons are easy. You may well be able to work in the community. There is day-leave! Week-end leave!

You can go into the local town and meet your girl. The staff in these places just

want a quiet life. They will turn a blind eye to an awful lot so long as you don't

cause any trouble. But if you continue talking to staff the way you are talking to

me then you will serve the whole three years. And if you act like this with other

inmates then you are asking for a razor across your face. And, incidentally.

Don't call me Mate.'

The man appeared even more annoyed. 'Do you know who I am?' he snarled

nastily.

I grinned. 'I don't have the faintest idea who you are,' I replied truthfully.

The man looked very surprised. 'I get new men in here every day,' I explained politely. 'All I am asking of you is reasonable behaviour.'

'I don't crawl to anyone,' he snarled indignantly. 'If people are funny with me, I just punch them. I don't care who he is,' he shouted loudly. He looked around my little office as if searching for someone to impress. It was unfortunate for him that I was on my own and I don't impress very easily. He certainly appeared to be in a bad mood. 'They call me 'the Big Fellah,' he boasted again.

'I can take anyone. Anyone at all. I don't give a fuck about anyone or anything.'

'Good,' I replied mildly, 'I'm glad you don't give a fuck. Because I don't give a fuck either.' I shoved a couple of forms across the desk at him. 'Sign them,' I ordered. 'And get out.'

He signed the forms, tossed them back at me, and stormed out. I grinned again.

'I will hear more of him,' I promised myself.

I did.

FIRST WING.

Apparently on his first wing several very interesting events occurred.

The man made a point of telling all the other inmates how hard and tough he

was, and the other cons listened with varying degrees of boredom and

disinterest. He quickly made himself very unpopular with both staff and

inmates.

During his first week he threatened an officer (Surprise! Surprise!) and the

screw pressed his First Response. When several more officers came running, 'the Big Fellah,' immediately backed off and started to apologise. 'It's all a

misunderstanding,' he expostulated. But when the Senior Officer informed him

that he was going to be 'nicked,' anyway for making threats this idiot raised his

fist again in a threatening manner. People learn behaviour patterns in life. Most

people learn their first behaviour patterns in school. Later, in life they learn such

patterns in work, with family, in social events and in the pub. In such situations

a person can usually threaten other people and get away with it. And if he gets a

reaction which appears too intense then he normally makes a joke out of and

backs down. Normally only actual physical contact triggers a fight. But jail is

different. To threaten a staff member is simply not acceptable. Immediately he raised his fist several prison officers jumped on him and twisted him up. This

man was then physically carried screaming and shouting to the Segregation

Unit. There are numerous stories about prison staff 'brutalising' inmates in such

circumstances. These stories are rubbish. There is absolutely no need at all to

brutalise anyone. The approved methods of Control and Restraint are far more

efficient. This was exactly what happened to him. An officer grabbed each arm

and placed the man in 'locks.' This simply means that his arms are twisted up

behind his back and his wrists are manacled. The inmate was then dragged,

carried, pushed and pulled to the Segregation Block. He was manhandled into a cell, forced onto the floor and his legs were twisted into a figure of four

position. Each arm was twisted up behind his back while an officer knelt on

each of his shoulder blades. Another officer held his head to stop him from

biting anyone. All of this is excruciatingly painful, and the pain is continuous

unlike a punch or kick where the pain only lasts for seconds. There is no need to

'brutalise' anyone. The pain is far worse when approved methods are used. This

is known as 'the therapeutic use of pain.' And the bonus is that it is all

completely legal. If the manager on duty feels it necessary, then the man can be

stripped naked. If he does not cooperate in undressing, then an extremely sharp

knife can be used to physically cut his clothes off until he is stark naked. Then the restraining officers then take it in turns to suddenly jump off the offender

until only the one holding his arms is left. This man then gives the man's arms a

wrench upwards which causes severe pain and then leaps backwards through

the open door which is instantly slammed into the prisoner's face. By the time

he has recovered from the pain he is all alone in a strip cell. He later appeared

before the visiting Magistrate and lost three weeks remission. In fact, I thought,

he was quite lucky.

After this incident he altered his attitude towards the screws.

But he was still quite obnoxious towards the inmates. Or rather towards some

inmates.

On this Wing there was one small, exceptionally undistinguished, looking inmate who kept very much to himself and did not bother anyone. This man was

in his late twenties but looked a lot younger. He was small, slightly built, and

inoffensive to everyone. He had been in custody since was a boy. The older

men all knew him well and many other inmates and staff knew him by

reputation. Every one of them was polite and courteous to him. Unlike the Big

Fellah they were not stupid.

The ordinary cons could have warned him about the little man, but no one

bothered.

'Why should we?' they asked each other. Several of them asked me this

question? Finally, of course the great day came.

One of the inmates who told me this story commented. 'We had all been waiting for this to happen Boss,' he explained gleefully. 'And at last it

happened.'

The inmates were queuing up for dinner when the big man pushed his way to

the front. Not one other person in the queue commented in any way or said

anything. Only the little man who simply stated truthfully, accurately and very

politely. 'Do you mind? I was ahead of you in the queue?'

The Big Fellah turned to him. 'Fuck off midget,' he stated nastily. 'Don't get

funny with me. I'm next!' The little man simply stood there and stared straight

at the big man. He did not utter one single word. 'I told you to fuck off,' the big

man snarled. 'Get funny with me and I'll hurt you really badly.'

The little man walked to the back of the queue while no-one either spoke or

moved. The Big Fellah laughed out loud while a couple of his sycophants in the

dinner queue laughed obediently. The big man scoffed his meal and swaggered

off. Later, that day the little man procured a razor, walked into the cell

belonging to the Big Fellah and slashed his face open. For some strange reason

not one single person on the wing witnessed this. Fortunately for the Big Fellah

he was not too badly injured. He was lucky. When he was asked who had

assaulted him, the so-called 'Big Fellah,' simply stated. 'I can't remember.'

He was starting to learn.

His education continued.

An unpleasant, prison practice is known as 'swilling.' Nothing complicated.

Just a procedure whereby any unpopular prison officer or inmate is drenched in

the contents of a chamber pot hurled over him from an upstairs landing. The pot

holds a mixture of urine, faeces, vomit, spittle, bleach, paint-thinners and any

possible available, anti-social substance. In female prisons used sanitary towels

are included.

A few days later 'the Big Fellah,' was strutting around the wing in his usual

arrogant, unpleasant manner when someone tossed the contents of a chamber

pot all over him. He was completely and thoroughly drenched. This procedure is

usually reserved for unpopular staff, but inmates are not prejudiced. They will

swill anyone. The Big Fellah was coated in a deep, rich, brown, foul-smelling broth of semi-liquid diarrhoea which dripped all over his face, clothes and body.

Staff and inmates of Her Majesty's Prisons are renowned for their tough sense

of humour. The entire wing, staff and inmates, roared with laughter.

After this it transpired that the 'Big Fellah,' as he liked to be called had earned

himself a brand-new nickname. Behind his back he was now known as,

'Shitface.' Some of the older, tougher men on the wing called him this to his

face. Apparently, he hated this nickname. Not surprisingly! The little man was

interviewed but firmly denied such a reprehensible act such as tossing urine and

faeces over another inmate. Apparently not one single person had witnessed it

happening. Surprise! Surprise! No-one cared anyway.

A Prison Officer told me the next story. He named a gang of infamous, Liverpool, criminal brothers who had all been in and out of Altcourse at various times and who were all well-known for violence. 'The word is that he annoyed one of them,' the Officer stated grimly.

'What was the word?" I asked. By now I was genuinely curious.

'They found him in a cell one day,' the officer explained. 'Someone had smashed his face in. He was rushed to the hospital wing.'

'So, what happened next?' I inquired.

'We asked him how he sustained the injuries and he said he fell down the stairs,' the officer laughed. Then the old screw looked at me and his face straightened out. 'Evidently his mother is an old age pensioner and they know where she lives,' he explained sadly. 'They promised him they would pour

petrol through her letter box if he said anything.' The officer shrugged

indifferently. 'He is starting to learn,' he commented sadly.

'Most people do,' I agreed, 'but some people are so stupid that it takes them a

lot longer than others.'

The screw gave a shrug. 'Nothing we can do about that,' he emphasised grimly.

'I gave him advice on how to behave. It is up to him to take it.'

MONTHS LATER.

I had forgotten all about this when some months later I visited the Enhanced

Wing and another officer indicated this same man to me. 'See that lad. He's as

good as gold now. No trouble at all.'

I recognised the man at once and recalled our first meeting. 'Good,' I agreed.

'I'm glad he's settled down and is behaving himself. What was he like when he first arrived?'

'He came from Canal Wing,' the screw elaborated. 'While he was there, he was one complete and utter pest. He wouldn't stop annoying people. Cons! Screws! All the other staff! He was one right pain in the backside.'

'So, what happened?" I asked curiously.

The officer laughed. 'He's learnt his lesson. He will be out soon. He's not a bad lad. He just needed to learn the rules. Now he's as good as gold. Just the type of fellah we want on an enhanced wing,' the officer laughed again. 'And he's the best Wing Cleaner we've ever had.'

After these episodes the man behaved himself impeccably. He changed his

attitudes and behaviour completely. Instead of strutting around the wing

throwing his weight around he crept and crawled along with the worst of them.

He was polite to a fault with the screws and crawled around after the so-called,

'Hard Men,' on the wing.

YEARS LATER.

Every fairy story has a hundred variations, but the central theme will always be

the same. Some novels and stories are so good that they have been copied ad

infinitum. Robinson Crusoe; the story of one man, or a small group of people all

alone against the elements. Treasure Island; the tale of a fortune buried in a far-off place. Ten Little Indians, the saga of a gang of people marooned in a remote

place and one of them is a psychopathic killer. Sherlock Holmes, the brilliant

detective with his bumbling but brave sidekick Doctor Watson. Every one of

these sagas have been endlessly imitated.

The most famous, prison, fairy story is something on the lines of. 'When I was

in jail no one messed with me. No One! No one touched me. Not staff. Not

cons! They all knew better.'

A variation of this are the famous lines uttered by Rodger Daltrey in the prison

movie, 'McVicar.' 'Alright I know I'm going to lose but I'll come the best

second you've ever seen.'

At this point in the movie, of course, the prison officers back down. In real life they don't.

Lots of times I have heard inmates repeat Daltrey's statement almost word for word. I once turned around to an inmate who uttered this and said. 'Write your own lines.'

To be fair one of his friends burst out laughing and said. 'So, you've seen the movie as well Boss?'

Ha! Ha! Ha!

One reason why the Prison Service receives such terrible publicity is because it is incredibly paranoid about publicity and many managers simply do not trust their own staff. Any staff who are likely to be interviewed by media representatives will be cautioned by their superiors and warned. 'Don't say anything. Not one word. Understand that if you do make any statements to the

media then that is a disciplinary matter?' Of course, staff have mortgages to

pay, children to feed, elderly relatives to care for. They cannot risk being

unemployed. Nurses cannot risk being struck off the Nursing Register.

The situation for ex-inmates is totally different. They couldn't care less. They

have nothing to lose. So, they go ahead and relate the most incredibly lurid and

exaggerated accounts of brutalities, beatings and any other far-fetched story that

will raise eyebrows. This sounds far better than the truth. And it is a great way

of getting revenge on the Prison Service which locked you up.

THE FAIRY STORY.

Some years later when memories of, 'the Big Fellah,' (AKA 'Shitface.') had

receded into my distant past, I sat in a Merseyside public house and the man

himself walked in. I recognised him instantly. He did not recognise me or even

see me. I was sitting in a corner alcove enjoying my drink and watching him. (I

always sit in a corner. If I can't sit in a corner, then I always sit with my back to

the wall. Whenever I walk into a bar or restaurant, I always find myself carrying

out a three hundred and sixty degree, all round surveillance of the entire room

and the people in it. Many police and prison staff and ex-staff do this. Funnily

enough so do lots of criminals.)

I sat and listened with great interest as the Big Fellah (AKA Shitface.) ordered a pint then stood up at the bar and talked in a very loud voice as he entertained the

bar with stories of his time inside. He related how 'all the screws were scared of

me.' He went on to describe and name various infamous criminals who he

claimed to have served time with. Incidentally one of the crooks he mentioned

was Curtis Warren who had never even been in Altcourse Jail. (CURTIS

WARREN; an infamous, Liverpool, drug dealer.) Evidently these men would

bully 'ordinary,' inmates. 'But they never messed with me,' Shitface boasted.

'They knew better.'

I watched as he glared around the bar looking for someone to impress and I

remembered that day in my office when he had done exactly this. It was like watching a bad movie, the second time round. And it was just as bad and just as

boring the second time.

'I don't take shit off anyone,' he bragged. I almost burst out laughing as I heard

this statement. He had certainly taken some shit off the little man whom he had

tried to push around. 'No one messes with me,' the Big Fellah insisted.

'The prisoners were all scared stiff of me. And the screws!'

Many times, I have sat in a bar and listened while some ex-inmate tells the

entire bar some such fairy story or other. This fairy story that the Big Fellah was

relating with such apparent truth and gusto was as far removed from the truth as

it is possible to be.

I glanced around the bar room to observe the reactions he was getting. Some people looked bored stiff. Others totally ignored him. Two lads in their teens

were, standing attentively hanging on to his every word. A couple of women

nudged their male companions, quietly picked up their handbags, finished their

drinks and walked out.

A young man and his girl approached me, carrying drinks and asked if there

was room for them. I moved over and we all sat together in the little alcove. The

young couple started chatting in a friendly and informal manner. It was all very

pleasant.

The door swung open and four, young men wearing motorcycle leathers and

carrying crash helmets barged in. They were all in their twenties and thirties and

all looked tough and fit. None of them had Scouse accents. I guessed that they were just passing through and wanted to relax after a long ride. They sat

together in one corner. The pub served bar snacks and they gratefully scoffed

meat pies, pasties, crisps, beers, listened to a bit of music, used the toilets and

freshened up. None of them were drinking heavily. One lad had a Coca-Cola. I

watched with great interest as the Big Fellah suddenly stopped talking and

turned his back on them.

Suddenly, the Big Fellah was a quite different person and I wondered exactly

what else had happened to him inside. One thing, and one simple thing, was for

sure. And I would bet money on this one simple fact. He would never tell a

living sole the true facts of exactly what had happened to him inside.

The motorbike gang drank up and left. They had been there for about twenty

minutes and in that time the Big Fellah had not uttered one single word except

to order a fresh pint.

As the little gang walked out the Big Fellah returned to his soliloquy.

'I remember when one of the screws got funny with me, he boasted. 'I just

belted him. It took six of the bastards to take me. But I made a right mess out of

three of them before they won. It was six to one. I could take any one of them,

man, to man. Afterwards I told them all. 'You touch me, and I'll get every

single one of you bastards on your own. 'They could push some people around

but not me. I never took any shit off anyone. Me, and my mates ran that prison.

The governor knew that if I said the word there would be a riot that would close

the whole place down. No one messes with me. No one.'

Men who make statements like this usually have deep-seated problems of their

own. We all remember the school bully who was usually the big, fat, ugly slob

who came bottom of the class and who had nothing else in life other than the

fact that he was, supposedly, 'hard and tough.' Just like this silly, inadequate,

Shitface who made life a misery for other smaller, weaker lads. The reason why

such a man acts like this is simple. It is gross inadequacy founded on an

inferiority complex. He compensates by bullying people who he perceives as

weaker than himself.

I was tempted to ask his two, teenage admirers what they thought of his sudden

change of behaviour when the Motorcycle Gang entered. I looked at them

carefully. One of them seemed to be completely oblivious to the situation. His

friend was a little older and he had a more intelligent look about him. He now

had a look of world-weary cynicism on his face. I grinned. 'You have just lost a

fan,' I thought to myself. The young couple who had sat with myself and my

lady friend looked disgusted and, quite frankly bored stiff.

The girl who was sitting with us turned to me. 'Have you ever met that fat slob

before?' she asked me as she gestured towards, 'the Big Fellah.'

'How would I know a man like that?' I asked innocently. 'Anyway, who is he?'

The girl gave a contemptuous snort then grinned. 'He's the village idiot,' she

explained. 'Just because he's been in jail, he thinks it is something to be

proud of,' she gave a dismissive and indignant snort. 'Lots of lads have been in

jail,' she commented accurately. 'But most of them never boast about it. In fact

most lads who have been in jail never tell anyone. Did you notice how he

suddenly shut up when those motorbike lads came in?' she gave another

cynical giggle. 'Everyone laughs at him, she explained. 'He is just a total and

utter idiot. Behind his back his nickname is 'Knobby.''

'Why is he called Knobby?' I asked curiously.

The girl laughed. 'See that woman over there,' she gestured at a well-built, good-looking, busty female standing at the bar. She looked about fifty and had

blond hair with black roots. She was wearing a tight, low-cut, black, mini dress

which showed off her good legs and big breasts along with black, high-heeled

shoes and lots of garish make-up. She was swilling gin and tonics. She looked

as if she was out on the pull. 'We call her Marty,' the girl explained. The girl

laughed again. 'Her name is really Linda. But we call her Marty.'

'Why?' I asked curiously.

'Don't you remember the old jingle, 'Any time! Any place! Anywhere!

Martini!' The girl laughed again. 'She is a very obliging lady,' she told me

cynically. 'Apparently one night she was blind, paralytic drunk and that idiot made a play for her. She told us that, at the time she was desperate, drunk and

lonely and felt like a shag. There was no one else available so she took him

back to her place.'

This young lady does not mince her words,' I thought to myself.

'So why is he called Knobby?' I asked curiously.

'Because when he dropped his pants, she realised instantly that he had

gonorrhoea.' The girl laughed out loud, 'Marty couldn't give a toss who knows

about her private life, so she told the entire pub that he had a dose. That is how

he got to be called Knobby. It is short for 'knobrot.' Again, the young girl

laughed. 'He told everyone he was going to give Marty a good hiding,' she explained. 'But the older men in this pub all told him that if he laid one finger

on her they would batter him.' The girl gave another cynical again. 'So much

for the big, tough hard case,' she sneered.

Just like the young lady I laughed out loud. My old mate was certainly in the

business of acquiring imaginative nicknames I thought.

Sometimes when you are in a situation like this and you listen to the sort of

drivel that this man was spouting you feel inclined to say something. But you

don't. Instead you just give a mental shrug and go back to enjoying your pint,

your food and the company of a pretty girl.

I sat and laughed quietly to myself as 'the Big Fellah,' told the world how hard

and tough, he was.

But not once did he mention being twisted up and restrained.

Nor did he tell people how he had his face slashed open.

Nor did he tell everyone about the other occasion when he had his face smashed

in.

Not once did he mention that his nickname inside was, 'Shitface.'

Nor did he explain how he had earned this nickname.

Mind you I would have been amazed if he had.

My new-found friend turned to me. 'What are you laughing at?' she asked

curiously.

I grinned. 'Nothing really,' I laughed. 'Just a private joke.'

Like I said, every good fairy story has a hundred variations.

This story was obviously getting better each time 'the Big Fellah,' AKA

'Shitface,' AKA 'Knobby,' told it.

And, not once did he mention what 'a really, good wing cleaner,' he had been.

As inmates go this man was an absolute classic.

THE PSYCHIATRIC PATIENT.

I met a patient in a Mental Health Unit who repeatedly and persistently

offended not only against all of the rules and regulations of the hospital but also

against the rules of decency and good behaviour. He went shoplifting, begging,

spent time hanging around public lavatories selling his body for immoral

purposes. He abused alcohol and illegal drugs in any amounts and in any available quantities. He frequently appeared in court charged with petty

offences. He continually pestered staff with unrealistic requests. On one

occasion he was visited by a Social Worker who asked him what his aims and

ambitions were. This man was a borderline subnormal who had literally dozens

of convictions and cautions for petty offences of theft and begging. He told her

that he would like to join the army. Fair enough! Anyone who works in

psychiatry gets used to completely unrealistic answers. But I have to say that I

was truly amazed when the social worker asked me afterwards what steps I was

taking to help him fulfil his ambition and become a soldier. I decided to tell her

the truth.

'The army would never touch him,' I explained. 'For a start he would never pass the medical. He has been abusing drugs for his entire life. He would not even get into an infantry battalion.'

The woman was very indignant. 'How do you know? It is his choice anyway. He should be allowed to make an attempt.'

I tried not to give an audible sigh. In this Nursing Home, we had one staff member with a car who was always obliging and helpful. I got him to escort this patient to the local Army Carers Office and drop the patient off outside. I also instructed him to watch the patient afterwards.

The patient got out of the car and looking into the window of the career office for about five minutes then wandered disconsolately off.

When I told the social worker the story, she suggested that we try again. I didn't

bother.

THE FIRST TIMER.

On one occasion I was admitting men to Altcourse Jail when a young lad came

through my door.

Sometimes a man struts in and tattooed across his fingers are the initials

ACAB and ASAB, and he sits down quite comfortably and asks. 'Hello Boss.

Are you the shrink?' Then he quite calmly eyes up the pretty, female, student

nurse who was with me. Then he looks around the little office and states. 'I'm

in for GBH Boss. But it's all a load of bollocks. It won't stand up in court. I'll be out of here in a couple of weeks. I've got a good brief. I'm gonna' walk.''

The other extreme is a man who nervously enters the room. His body language,

frightened facial expression, slumped-over posture and poor eye contact all give

away the fact that he is scared. His walk totally lacks the confident swagger of

the old lag. Even his language is different. He does not use jail argot.

Sometimes the situation was not so clear, but I found myself proficient in

assessing if a man was a First Timer or had been inside before. Some reasons

are clear and obvious as I have just described. Other situations are more

complicated. Imagine a customs man watching a line of people passing

through an airport. The customs official has been in the job for thirty years. For no apparent reason he picks a person out and orders his colleagues to search the

man. It turns out that the traveller is trying to smuggle something. If asked why

he decided to pick on this person he might say many things such as. 'It was the

way he walked.' 'He looked nervous.' 'He looked too confident.' 'He was

sweating.'

All these reasons may well be true, but the real reason is deeper and more

profound and it can be summed up in one word. The word is EXPERIENCE.

You can teach anyone knowledge. You cannot teach experience.

When I practised psychiatry in the prison service, I developed the same skills as

the customs man I have just described.

When this young lad entered my office that day, I knew instantly that he was a

First Timer. He sat down nervously, and as I started the interview the lad

relaxed slightly and asked me the two classic questions which I have been asked

thousands of times by new men.

'Will I get beaten up?" and, 'Will I get raped?'

'This is a good jail,' I explained. 'So long as you behave yourself her you will

be alright.' The lad seemed to listen to and to accept my advice. He relaxed

slightly and seemed to cheer up considerably. I called one of the Trusty's over

and introduced him. 'Have a chat with this lad please,' I requested. 'Show him

the ropes. This is his first time inside.'

'Glad to help Boss,' the Trusty replied.

When I got back to the Hospital Unit one of the girls asked me to accept a phone call. It was this lad's mother and she was desperately upset. She had

phoned Altcourse Jail and somehow or other been put through to me.

Apparently when her son went to court his relatives and friends all expected a

non-custodial sentence, but the judge gave him six months. According to his

mother he was mentally ill. He had tried to kill himself and he should be

immediately transferred to a mental hospital. I tried to explain to the upset lady

that the chances of her lad being sent to a Mental Unit were zero and that I

would not recommend this anyway. He had been sentenced to six months and as

this was his first time inside and as it was for a non-violent offence, he would

serve two months. Plus, for good measure the day was Monday which is the best day to be sent to jail on. You cannot be released on a Saturday or Sunday,

so, you will be released on a Friday which means that you automatically get two

days extra remission. Another bonus is that he would be able to claim back any

days he had spent in police cells. And in custody a part of a day is counted as a

full day. So, as this boy had been arrested at 22.10pm and released at 02.50am

then he had technically been in custody for two days. Which meant that, with

remission, he could claim back four days. And on his last day he is simply given

breakfast and a travel warrant to any reasonable place in the UK and discharged.

With any luck on his last day he would be out before dinner. I even made a

point of explaining to her that in the unlikely event of his being transferred to a

Mental Health Unit he could end up spending years there whereas if he behaved

himself, he should be out of prison in weeks rather than months. I also told her

that he had already been assessed by a Mental Health Nurse and would see a

Doctor first thing tomorrow morning.

'He may well have seen a nurse,' the lady protested vigorously. 'But you don't

seem to understand. He must see a Doctor.' Again, this is a very common

behaviour pattern with many people. Even in this modern day and age they still

assume that, 'the nurse,' is the little girl who runs and fetches and carries and

makes cups of tea for the Doctor. In Altcourse Prison the Doctors would refer

patients to R.M.N.'s like myself and ask us for a psychiatric opinion.

I felt very sorry for the lady and I tried to be kind to her. 'I have already booked him an appointment,' I explained again gently. 'He will see a Doctor first thing in the morning.'

The lady started crying. 'But that means he will spend the night in jail,' she protested.

There is an old saying. 'She didn't listen to a word I said.'

Mummy had obviously not listened to one word that I said. She was under the mistaken impression that when her son saw a Doctor, he would immediately be transferred to hospital.

In situations like this you may well feel sorry for the people you are talking to, but you simply should not make unrealistic promises. Some staff members do.

They will say things such as, 'Well he will see the Doctor in the morning. It is

up to him.'

The caller then thinks to herself. 'Everything will be alright.'

Some young man tells a girl. 'I think you are really attractive. I want to see

you again. I want you to be my girlfriend. In fact, let's get engaged. In the

meantime, take your knickers off.' Sometimes she believes him and takes her

knickers off. When she gets pregnant, he then indignantly denies ever saying

any such thing.

Also, just to complicate matters, some people, prison staff included, people have a habit of saying whatever it is that they think that the person listening to

them wants to hear. I have never done this. If a staff member does this then it is

only a short-term solution. If I had promised this lady a hospital transfer for her

son, or even the possibility of a hospital transfer then it would have simply

given both unrealistic and false hopes. In the short term this might be an easy

answer but in the long run a Prison Official is far better off giving the bad news

out straight away. Then if there is better news then this is an unexpected and

welcome bonus. Plus, I don't believe in telling lies anyway.

The next day I made a point of visiting the new lad before his Doctor's

appointment. He was sitting in his cell chatting, drinking tea and smoking with three other inmates. They all seemed relaxed and cheerful. I asked his new

friends to give me a couple of minutes and they obliged. 'He's alright Boss,'

one of them commented cheerfully. 'We're all from the same town. And we

all support the same football team.'

The new lad chatted freely. The suicide attempt was ten years previously. His

mental illness was depression. In prison depression simply cannot be recognised

as a mental illness. As I used to tell inmates. 'You are supposed to be depressed.

It is called punishment.' Even after one night in jail and several conversations

with other prisoners he was already accepting his situation. I asked him to

phone his mother and tell her what had happened. He promised to do this. This lad was lucky. He met some decent inmates and made friends with lads who

helped him a lot. He did his time quietly and was discharged from prison. And

no! He was not transferred to a psychiatric hospital. I also spoke to his new-

found friends and asked them to give him advice on how to behave. They

promised to do this. Contrary to popular belief most inmates dislike bullying

intensely. Everybody remembers his first time and most grown men are mature

enough to be kind to the, 'new boy.' The exceptions to this rule are teenage

malcontents who have not the maturity or intelligence to recognise the hurt and

harm they are causing and the out and out psychopath who gets a kick out of

hurting and humiliating others. Several weeks later I did a follow up with this lad and he thanked me sincerely for making sure that he had NOT been

transferred to a mental hospital. By then he had heard to a litany of horror

stories, all true, about inmates who had spent years in such places after having

been convicted of trivial crimes and had then been transferred back to jail to

finish their sentences.

THE PAD THIEF.

I was once reading an inmate's Wing File when I saw a comment written by a

Prison Officer which stuck very firmly in my mind. 'This man is the lowest of

the low,' it read, 'He is a pad thief.' In jail of course a pad is a person's cell and

a pad thief is another inmate who steals from one of his colleagues. It is both interesting and rather hilarious that prisoners, who may have personally

stolen hundreds, perhaps thousands, of pounds, of money and property in their

life genuinely feel that for another person to steal from 'them,' is both

'different,' and 'wrong.'

I walked onto a wing. A new lad approached me He was unknown to me. 'Can I

have a word with you, Boss?' he asked. He appeared very angry.

'What can I do for you?' I inquired politely.

The lad started to explain. He was highly indignant. 'Some bastard has been in

my pad,' explained. 'My tobacco has been stolen. And my after shave. And a

chocolate bar.' The inmate pointed at the two prison officers who were sitting at

the console grinning broadly. 'Those two bastards just laughed at me,' he declared indignantly. 'They seem to think it is funny.'

One officer approached me. 'Hello Chris,' he greeted me. 'How are you?'

'I'm very well, thank you,' I replied. 'How are you?'

The officer indicated the youngster. 'Someone stole this lad's property,' he

explained with a huge grin.

Two other inmates, both older men joined our little group. One of the inmates

turned to the young lad again. 'What are you in jail for?' he asked.

The kid did not hesitate. 'I'm in for burglary,' he boasted proudly.

'How many? 'the man asked.

'They proved over a hundred,' the lad replied. 'But I've been burgling houses

since I was eleven years old.'

'Do you think it is really is terrible when a man breaks into your pad when

you are not even there and steals your possessions?' the prison warder asked

calmly.

Again, the lad looked angry. 'You all seem to think that this is a huge bloody

joke,' he stated emphatically.

THE RUGBY PLAYER.

One quiet Saturday morning I admitted five men to jail. The first four of them

were nonces, and all of them had committed offences of gross indecency with

small children. The last new inmate was a big, well-built lad dressed in a rugby

shirt. I did not know what he was charged with, but I knew that he was not a sex offender. 'Are you a rugby player?' I inquired.

The lad looked at me in surprise. 'Yes, as a matter of fact I am,' he agreed. 'I

play as right prop.'

'That was my position in my rugby days,' I told him. We spent about twenty

minutes chatting about rugby. It was a quiet day and he was cheerful company. I

completed the full physical, mental and social assessment that is completed with

every new admission. It was his first time inside. I gave him the usual advice,

shook hands and wished him all the best.

He was a heroin smuggler.

'Just how far down the social scale I have slipped?' I thought to myself

after they had all gone. 'When a heroin smuggler makes a pleasant change?'

MY FIRST EVER.

FIRST RESPONSE.

My first ever 'first response, 'occurred during my first month in jail. An

aggressive young man requested a doctor's app (appointment) and when he met

her, he spent the next ten minutes requesting, repeating, demanding, begging,

pleading and threatening as he asked for, 'medication,' to 'cure,' him. This

doctor was very friendly with me and she asked me to explain to him exactly

why she would not prescribe him medication. Quite what illness he had that he

needed treatment for was something he was not sure of. Nevertheless, he was certain that he needed 'tablets.' This is common behaviour in jail and is seen

again, and again. Jail is very claustrophobic and boring and the chance to get

high or low cannot be missed. This youngster fitted the mould which will be

familiar to readers of these stories. He was from the typical, dysfunctional,

background which characterises these boys. He talked constantly of crooks and

crimes, of girls and gambling, of football and fighting, of alcohol and drugs.

He himself was tall, slim athletic and looked like a useful lad in a punch up. By

and large one, more unpleasant, young lad from the one of inner cities of a

Northern Town.

I sat with him and talked politely and patiently to as I explained that he had no mental illness there was no reason to prescribe him medication. As usually

happens in such situations we kept on going around and around in circles with

both of us endlessly repeating ourselves.

Outside of jail if you are aggressive enough, persistent enough and/or nasty

enough and if you pester people enough you will usually get whatever it is that

you want.

I once met an inmate who started a big argument in his local Supermarket. He

swore that the cashier had short-changed him. He insisted that she had given

him change from a five-pound note when really, he had handed her a twenty.

When he complained the Manger was called, the till was checked and was

found to be correct. He was told, 'nothing can be done.' He argued and complained. The Manger still refused to do anything and, eventually called the

police. The man was forcibly removed. The next day he returned, stood in the

main entrance foyer and began slashing his arms with a razor blade while, at the

same time, shouting out that the Supermarket had swindled him. The police

were called, and again he was forcibly removed. The next day he returned again

at the shop's busiest rush hour, took a razor out and started slashing his wrists

and arms while still shouting his complaints to the entire world, staff and

customers included. At this point the Manager approached him and gave him

the disputed fifteen pounds simply in order to get rid of this ridiculous situation

which was causing so much trouble and disturbance and was upsetting customers and staff. Basically, most people will not create that much difficulty

over fifteen pounds.

But this man did, and the lesson here is clear. If you are prepared to cause

enough trouble, then at some point most people will back down and you will get

your own way. The inmate who told me this story was very proud of the fact

that he had won his case. He then told me that he had really given the cashier a

five-pound note and the whole story was a flat lie.

When I asked him why he did this he just laughed and boasted. 'Well I was with

a gang of my friends and we were drinking in the pub. We had this argument. I

bet them ten pounds each that I could make a big supermarket pay up in a situation like this. We all put money on the table and asked the publican to hold

the money for us. He thought it was a huge joke. I told my pals that if I caused

enough trouble then I would get the money. I had nothing better to do and it was

an easy way to get fifteen pounds off the shop,' he grinned. 'And I made

another forty pounds off my friends.'

I suppose if you have nothing better to do then it is an easy way to make

fifty-five pounds.

That day in the Prison Health Centre I spent three quarters of an hour explaining

matters to this young lad who wanted tablets. At the end of that time I asked

him politely if we could call the meeting to a close as we were not achieving

anything.

His reaction was to lose his temper and start shouting and swearing at me. I was

not particularly surprised or frightened. 'Come on now,' I suggested. 'We are

not getting anywhere with this conversation. The doctor will not prescribe you

anything and she has explained why. I have also spent forty-five minutes

explaining these matters to you.'

'Look Boss,' he snarled nastily. 'I am not budging from this chair until I get

tablets.'

'Don't be like that,' I remonstrated mildly. 'It won't get you anywhere.'

At this point the lad got angry and snatched up my pen. The idea of using a pen

as a weapon sounds like a French farce but, if a pen is rammed into your face it

can cause quite a nasty wound. I decided to give this boy another chance. After all I reasoned to myself. I had nothing to lose by trying. 'Look,' I explained

calmly. 'Put that pen down and walk quietly back to your wing and I will forget

that this has happened. If you don't stop this behaviour you will be twisted up

and placed on a charge and you will be in even more trouble. You are already

on remand for armed robbery. Come on now. Do yourself a favour.'

At that point I honestly expected this young lad to back down, apologise, and

perhaps offer to shake hands. I was soon disillusioned. The lad lunged at me

with the pen in a threatening manner. I couldn't believe his stupidity. I backed

off into the corridor and found that I was up against a locked door. Another staff

member was standing there. 'Would you press your First Response please?' I asked him politely.

Murphy's Law ensued that the man had just arrived in Healthcare and had not

yet reported his new location. The First Response Team of course all ran like

hell, to his previous location.

While he stood there threatening me a heated debate was taking place over the

airways as to where exactly where and what the first response was? The debate

continued as to if it was a genuine first response or a false alarm.

I have to say that in my subsequent years in jails all over Britain I never saw

this kind of shambles again.

'Is this a false alarm?' was asked several times over the radio. I could hear this

question being asked echoing from other people's radios.

'No, it is not a false alarm,' I snarled nastily. 'It is a genuine emergency.' While all of this was going on the lad faced me and several times made rather half-hearted lunges at me. I debated with myself as to if I should kick him in the testicles. I decided against it. In prison a member of staff can use as much force as they consider necessary in the situation. But if you do injure an inmate then afterwards in the calm, cool, collected atmosphere of a court room or the office of an inquiry you may well have to justify your actions before a panel of people who may have no sympathy for you at all! 'No, it is not a false alarm,' I snarled nastily. 'It is a genuine emergency.' While all of this was going on the lad faced me and several times made rather half-hearted lunges at me. I debated with myself as if I should kick him in the testicles. I decided against it. In prison a

member of staff can use as much force as they consider necessary in the

situation.

But if you do injure an inmate then afterwards in the calm, cool, collected

atmosphere of a court room or the office of an inquiry you may well have to

justify your actions before a panel of people who may have no sympathy for

you at all! Some senior people are great and are very understanding of the

problems which prison staff and psychiatric nurses face. Some could not care

less. And there is always the odd idiot who will believe every word which the

patient or inmate states and disbelieve every word the staff member says. 'Many a time I have stood and listened while a skilled liar who is an inmate or patient

will give his highly coloured account of an event and a nurse or staff will do

their best to tell the truth and make a bad job of it. I have had a doctor say to me

to my face. 'I believe that the truth lies halfway between these two accounts.'

In psychiatric hospitals in days gone by it was said, 'there are two types of

doctors.

There are those who you will run to help in case of trouble.'

The next question would be. 'What is the other kind of doctor?'

The answer is. 'The other type of doctor is one who, if they are attacked, you

run for help.'

Running for help might take an awful long time.

At last the First Response Team arrived and a manager stepped forward.

In hospitals most episodes of violence are appallingly badly managed and there

are many reasons for this. Hospitals are built, staffed and structured with one

concept in mind. The concept of giving care to sick people.

Jails are also built with one concept in mind. The idea is to lock up, control

and discipline people who are guilty of, or are accused of, breaking the law. In

hospitals also, there tend to be several different people who think they are in

charge.

I personally witnessed a violent episode in a General Hospital where a doctor,

several senior nurses, a couple of porters, a hospital administrator as well as a police officer where all trying to, 'help me,' calm down one patient. While I

was trying to calm down this one, old man, a group of these people were

standing at a safe distance shouting contradictory advice and instructions at me.

Many years ago, Napoleon famously said. 'One bad general is better than two

good ones.' In other words, there is nothing worse than a divided command.

That day in Altcourse Jail as soon as the team arrived, I knew I could relax. The

Senior Manager weighed the situation up in one second flat then turned to me.

'What's the problem?' he asked tersely.

I indicated the young prisoner who was standing facing me and holding my pen

in a threatening manner. 'This young man has my pen,' I explained. 'And he

has threatened to stab me with it.'

The Senior Officer spoke to me quickly and concisely. 'Back off please,' he

ordered. I did exactly that. The Senior Man turned to several other nursing staff.

'Go to another room please?' he requested calmly and politely.

The fewer witnesses there are to a violent episode the better. An inmate who has

an audience has the temptation to play up. Also, if there are no witness' then he

can back down without loss of face.

The Manger faced the youngster. 'Look lad,' he explained reasonably. 'There

are four of us. There is one of you. If it comes to violence you are going to lose.

Now put that pen down and apologise to Mr Kinealy and you can walk back to

your wing. If you do that then we will not even take this matter any further.

Alright!'

It is interesting to note that this manager tried the, 'soft option,' first.

I asked him afterwards if he would have kept this promise if the inmate had obeyed orders. He assured me that he would have. This manager of course, was not aware that I had already tried this technique. In effect this lad was given two chances instead of one.

'Fuck off,' the young lad replied. 'I'm going nowhere. Not until I get my tablets.'

I watched with great interest. The manger looked around and addressed the staff. 'Are you ready?' he asked. They gave affirmative nods. He spoke to the lad once more. 'Alright!' he concluded. 'Last chance. I am giving you a direct order. Drop that pen! Now!'

'Fuck off,' was the succinct reply.

The manager turned to his team and spoke again. 'Alright lads?' he asked.

There were three affirmative nods. The Manger spoke again. 'RUSH HIM!' he shouted. 'NOW!'

In novels and films the gang always obligingly attack the hero one as a time. In real life they always act simultaneously. First Response Teams always win, and inmates always lose. In seconds this lad was on the floor with his arms twisted up behind his back screaming out loud. 'You are hurting me! You are hurting me!'

A 'freeze all movement,' was called and silly boy was escorted to the Segregation Unit.

Months later I met him again and he shook hands with me as he apologised for

his actions that day. 'I just got five years for armed robbery Boss,' he told me

with a huge smile. 'I'm really pleased. I was expecting at least ten years.'

I shook hands and wished him the best of luck.

What a waste!

TRANSFER TO A MENTAL HOSPITAL.

When inmates get their wish and are transferred to a Mental Health

Hospital there are certain procedures which must be carried out. Right up until

the actual time that a hospital official has signed and accepted responsibility for the prisoner he is still technically and legally the responsibility of the Prison

Service. This was in the days when 'private prisons' were still something of a

joke and we all knew how careful we had to be.

On one occasion I escorted a man to a Mental Health Unit. He was delighted to

be going and I anticipated no trouble. Such a transfer requires an armoured

security van, a driver and a couple of screws. Also, a trained nurse as an escort.

When I started in Altcourse there was an on-going debate as to whether the

nurse should be an RMN or an RGN. I was delighted to explain that since I was

doubly qualified this was no problem. I always volunteered to be the Nurse

Escort for such transfers. I like to visit new places and have new experiences.

Some of the places I went to were fascinating. Rampton Special Secure Unit was in a class of its' own. It was amazing.

When we got to the Hospital, I left the wagon and took the paperwork to the Ward Office. I introduced myself and explained the purpose of my visit. 'Would you sign here please,' I requested politely. 'And then he is all yours.'

The Nurse in charge looked at me as if I had crawled out from a sewer. Often some NHS staff, (not all of them by any means) look down on Prison Nurses and Doctors. We are regarded as lesser beings by some such staff.

'I can't sign anything,' this nurse informed me curtly.

In a job like mine you get used to difficult people. 'What is the problem?' I asked.

'I can't sign anything until we have accepted the patient,' he replied bad temperedly.

It seemed that this man was having a bad day. 'Alright,' I agreed. 'I will go and get him.'

We handcuffed the new patient to an officer and marched him through the hospital to the Ward Office. Once again, I proffered the paperwork. 'Sign here,' I requested. 'He is all yours now.'

The nurse looked at me in complete and utter disgust. 'You have just marched a patient right through this hospital in handcuffs,' he asserted angrily. 'Do you not have any respect for his dignity?'

'Look lad!' I replied, just as angrily. 'You point blank refused to accept the man. If we had escorted him here without handcuffs and he had run off and

escaped, you would be screaming about our negligence.'

We had quite an unpleasant argument and we disagreed.

MANY MONTHS LATER.

I was escorting another inmate to the same hospital and to the same ward. I had

the same driver. 'Wait here please,' I requested wearily.

Once again, I entered the same Ward office and explained myself. Another

person was on duty and this nurse could not have been more pleasant. This

man introduced himself by name, invited us all to sit down, made us all a cup of tea, explained where the Gents was sited and chatted cheerfully. 'You

have a choice,' I explained politely. 'I can march the prisoner through the

hospital in handcuffs and you can sign the documents in this office here. Or, if

you prefer it you can come to the wagon and sign there and escort the man in

yourself. Or, if you prefer it you can sign for the man in the wagon and we will

escort him in here. Or you can refuse to accept the man because you are not

happy with any of these options. But please realise that, the moment you sign

those documents he is legally yours.'

The nurse in charge looked at me in surprise.

'Is there some problem?' he asked.

I grinned. 'Well what's it to be?' I asked.

The nurse looked at me narrowly. 'Have you had problems here in the past?' he

inquired again.

'I sure have,' I agreed cheerfully. I related the story and the attitudes of the

nurse whom I had met on my previous visit. The new man gave an exasperated

shrug then stood up and shook hands with me. 'Sorry about that my friend,' he

apologised seriously. 'We all have to work with idiots in every place.'

Before we left, I shook hands with the patient and wished him the best of luck.

I also shook hands with all the staff and thanked them.

These people were all polite, professional and friendly.

Same hospital!

Same ward!

Different day!

Different staff!

What a difference.

THE GOOD SAMARITANS.

The British prison population is becoming increasingly older. There are many

reasons for this. The population generally is becoming older. Better medication,

better nutrition, less use of tobacco, more awareness of the need for training and

fitness; the list is endless. Another clear-cut reason is that hanging has been

abolished so many inmates die in jail simply out of old age. And even with

generous remission sentences nowadays are much longer. Old people die more

frequently than young people.

People die in police stations. Sometimes indeed there may well have been a

vicious fight and force has been used. But police and prison staff have a legal

and moral right to defend themselves.

Every so often a prisoner in a jail, police station or other custodial establishment

attempts suicide. Every so often he/she succeeds and when they do then there is,

'an inquiry.' If any person dies in any kind of custody in Great Britain, then by

law there must be an inquiry. And even if a person dies, for any reason

whatsoever, within seventy-two hours of being discharged from any kind of

police or prison custody then there still must be an inquiry. If the person was

still inside at the time of death, then usually the media and the family make lurid claims that their loved one was brutalised and mistreated by custody staff and

that a 'cover-up,' or 'whitewash,' is taking place. There will be claims that the

pleas for help from the prisoner and his family were ignored.

As one would expect this is utter rubbish. To seriously suggest that prison

officers would assault an inmate and murder him just for fun, or because they

dislike him is simply ridiculous. The people who make these allegations do not

have the faintest idea about the internal discipline or the rules and regulations

and infra structure of modern prisons. When the notorious murderer Harold

Shipman was found hanged in his cell claims of this sort were made. And this

was a horrible, mass murderer whose idea of fun was cold-bloodedly killing, innocent old ladies. His family were understandably upset at Shipman's death

but to expect the general public to agree with them and feel the same way is a

bit much.

On a prison night shift no-one other than an acting manager has any cell keys.

This rule is based on hard experience. It has happened that some inmates have

pretended suicide and arranged themselves in dramatic poses to persuade staff

to panic and open the cell door. It is human nature when a person sees another

man or woman in desperate need to rush to their help. The inmate can then

assault the staff member steal their keys and attempt escape. So now the very

strict rule is that if a member of staff needs to open a cell of a night then they must summon a manager and three prison officers must be present when the cell

is unlocked. If it is a two-man cell, then six prison officers must be present. This

rule is easy to enforce because only the Night Manager has cell keys. Also, a

nurse or Doctor must be present. To suggest that a manager, three prison

officers and a nurse will collude together to murder an inmate in these

circumstances is nothing short of incredible. Five people, some of whom hardly

know each other, or may perhaps never even met before, must be present.

And the subsequent inquiry will often fail to distinguish between two totally

different issues. There is the genuine suicide in which the person really wants to

die and a 'para-suicide,' which is a suicidal gesture posed to achieve some aim or other and which then simply goes wrong but results in death. Shipman clearly

intended to kill himself. As an ex-trained doctor, he would have good specialist

knowledge on exactly how to do this.

I met a man who loaded a double-barrelled, twelve-bore shotgun, shoved it into

his mouth and pulled both triggers. Now THAT is what I call attempted suicide.

(Amazingly enough this man survived.) On the other extreme many people will

scratch their wrists, place ligatures around their necks and make threats of

suicide. Usually they then press their emergency buzzers. But every so often

something goes wrong, and the person dies. This is then classed as a 'suicide.'

But it is not suicide at all. It is para-suicide, or a cry for help, which went wrong. Another problem is, 'the little boy who cried wolf.' Each cell has an

alarm buzzer. These bells are supposed to be there for an emergency. In real life

of course, inmates press them to demand instant attention at any hour of the day

or night for anything and everything imaginable. And just to complicate matters

many inmates make requests or which the nurse, prison officer or other official

simply cannot give. Then when the demand is refused the prisoner will

shout out loudly in front of as many witnesses as possible something on the

lines of; 'If I don't get what I want I will kill myself.' It is patently obvious that

this statement is rubbish. The man who really wants to die makes no threats at

all. He just goes off very quietly and commits suicide.

I once attended an inquest in which an inmate had wrapped a ligature around his

neck. He then pressed his alarm. But a disturbance broke out as he did so and by

the time prison staff attended his cell, he was dead. The unfortunate fact is that

once you are either dead or unconscious you cannot change your mind. You are

stuck with the decision. And even if a person has made dozens of different

attempts at so-called suicide prior to this then this is still classed as suicide. In

reality of course, it was not suicide at all. And, just to complicate matters you must distinguish between suicide attempts

and self-harm. In prison many people slash themselves, jump off balconies, stub

cigarettes out on their own arms and legs and carry out self-harming acts for a variety of reasons.

In the case in point I met a young lad who tried to hang himself. It was a serious attempt. One of his friends happened to visit his cell as this happened. The boy screamed for help and when a second young inmate came running, he told the lad to fetch the screws. In this case the rescuer held the victim up so that the pressure of the noose eased off and supported him until the prison officers arrived. (Every prison official carries a 'fish knife,' on his belt and this is specifically designed to cut through ligatures. It is always preferable to cut the noose in such cases because if there is a suspicion of foul play a knot could be vital evidence. I personally carried a fish knife every day for twelve years in

Altcourse Prison and I used it just once. (In my last few months!) The staff cut

the lad down and undoubtedly saved his life.

I made a point of visiting the rescuers on the wing and spoke to them. I thanked

them both but the one lad was upset himself. He spoke to me quite bitterly. 'We

have been getting a lot of stick over this case Boss,' he confided. 'The other

lads are saying that we had no right to interfere. They are saying that if he

wanted to kill himself then that was his affair. They are saying it was none of

our business.'

'They are talking absolute and utter rubbish,' I emphasised. They both looked at

me and obviously needed some reassurance. 'Have either of you ever thought

about killing yourselves?' I asked.

They both pondered for a moment until one lad spoke. 'Well about a year ago

Me and my bird split up,' he admitted. 'And I was really depressed. I had been

going with her ever since I was a kid. But she found out that I'd been shagging

her best mate. So, she finished with me. I was really depressed for a long time.

Then one night me and my mates went out and I copped off with some other

piece of stuff and I spent the night with her.' The lad grinned openly. 'My mum

and dad were on holiday that week,' he boasted. 'We went back to my place.

And I ended up in bed with her. The next day I felt totally different,' he

allowed. 'When I walked down to the shop next morning, I felt great. The sun

was shining, and the birds were singing,' he quoted solemnly.

I grinned back. 'You take my point then,' I pointed out. 'Every man who ever

lived has been there,' I pointed out truthfully. I shook hands with both lads.

'Have you ever felt suicidal Boss?' one lad asked curiously.

Sometimes in the job like that you had to think very hard before answering

certain questions. It is bad policy in jail, or for that matter in psychiatry, to give

away too much of your private life, but sometimes common sense prevails. 'In

point of fact I have,' I admitted. 'I think just about everybody has at some time

or another. But always remember the golden rule. If you do kill yourself then

you can't change your mind afterwards but if you wait for matters to improve

then life could get better.'

They both laughed at these pearls of wisdom.

'Listen to me,' I ordered. 'You two are both good lads and I am proud of you

both. What is more I am going to make an entry into both of your Wing Files,

about how you saved your friend's life?'

They looked at me in surprise. 'Are you really going to do that?' one boy asked.

'I never make promises that I don't keep,' I answered seriously.

I did keep this promise.

TWENTY-EIGHT DAYS!

A new man came into the jail. He was about fifty years old but looked fit and

agile. He had just received twenty-eight days. It was a Monday afternoon. 'How

long will I serve Boss?' he asked anxiously.

I figured quickly. 'You will serve fourteen days out of that stretch,' I explained.

'It is almost six 'o' clock now but today will be classed as your first day. And

you will be released next Friday morning. So, you will only serve ten full days.'

I expected the man to be pleased but he seemed very annoyed.

'Can't I do the whole stretch?' he asked.

I was curious, and the man explained. 'I met this young bird recently,' he

explained. 'She is nineteen years old and not much to look at. But she has a

body on her like Samantha Fox and she is sex mad. We've been screwing like

bunny rabbits.'

I could not help but grin. 'What's the problem then?' I asked.

The man thought for a moment and then spoke. 'I'm fifty-five years old Boss,' he confided. 'I've been having a great time. But I am absolutely knackered. I'm

dead beat. I just need a break.'

I laughed out loud. 'Just give her telephone number to some of the lads who are

due out soon,' I suggested. 'By the sound of her they will be only too glad to

oblige her. They should keep her happy until you are released.'

The new inmate was a typical man. 'I don't want her shagging other fellahs,'

he protested indignantly. 'She's my bird. I don't want anyone else going near

her.'

I was tempted to say. 'You can't have it both ways,' but I didn't bother.

I was also tempted to say. 'I doubt if a sex-mad nineteen years old girl will wait

a whole month for you. By the time you get out she will probably be forgotten you even exist.'

I didn't say any of this. I just shook hands and wished him the best of luck.

Apparently, he went around telling the prison staff to fuck off at every

opportunity and got 'nicked,' numerous times. He always pleaded guilty at the

hearings and told the Prison Director or the Home Office official to fuck off as

well. He lost his remission and served the entire stretch.

A few weeks later another inmate who had been very friendly with the man told

me the rest of the story.

'What happened was this Boss,' his friend confided in me. 'Apparently when he finally got out and returned home, he found his house occupied by a gang of

young lads who were all smoking drugs and drinking beer. His expensive colour

television, DVD recorder, collections of DVDs and his other possession had all

disappeared. Even a lot of his furniture had gone. His girlfriend was now his

'ex-girlfriend.' He found her in his bed, in his bedroom, in his house, with two

different lads at the same time. Meanwhile a gang of other lads were sitting

downstairs waiting their turn. He lost his temper and told them all to get out.

They laughed in his face and eventually it came to violence. He lost the fight, so

he went to a nearby pub and called the police. By the time that the police

arrived, the young lads who he had the fight with had all gone, and he was able to furnish only the vaguest of descriptions of the ones who had assaulted him.

The other lads all swore blind that they did not know these other lads. In fact,

they knew nothing about anything. But all of them had seen him attack several

lads. His 'girlfriend,' was still there though, and the man agreed that he had

given her permission to stay. The remaining boys all insisted that they were just

sitting their drinking coffee. The girl denied all knowledge of his missing

possessions. His insurance company refused to pay him anything because he

had given the girl permission to live there. His house was a complete and utter

shambles.'

He walked away from the situation a poorer, weaker, wiser man.

Still at least he had a good time with her.

I wonder though, on sober reflection, he thought it was all worth it.

I doubt it.

A FUNNY STORY!

I once met two young lads who totally fitted the description of 'scally,' which is

jail argot for scallywag. They were both skinny scrawny and scruffy with old

track marks down their arms. The reason why such lads are always skinny and

scruffy is because drug addicts spend all their money on drugs. Heroin is an

appetite suppressant anyway and junkies cannot be bothered wasting money on

non-essential luxuries such as food, clothing and rent. Funnily enough I quite

liked them both. Their saving graces were a sense of humour and an endless stack of funny stories. Many such lads chat to you and as you build up a rapport

with them you sometimes you say to yourself, 'there but for the grace of God,

go I.' When you remember your own childhood and contrast it with the stories

that these lads tell you do not wonder why such boys are in jail. The amazing

thing is that MORE of them are not in jail.

I was standing by the Wing Console chatting casually with these two boys.

There were two screws and three cons also present.

One youngster pontificated on about his crimes and seemed quite proud of his

past escapades.

At some point I interjected with a casual reprimand. 'It's all very well telling

me all about what you have done,' I pointed out, 'but the negative side of this is that you are both locked up and you can't go for a beer. You can't have sex with

your girlfriend. You can't play football without permission. In fact, you can't

even go for a walk in the park.'

The taller and older of the two thought carefully for a moment and then spoke.

'Maybe that is right Boss,' he replied. 'But you must remember that we've lived

the high life.'

We all considered him for a moment, and then I spoke. 'Exactly what have you

done in 'the High Life,' that was so great?' I asked. I was actually genuinely

curious.

Both lads laughed out loud. 'We sell drugs Boss. Everyone knows who we

are. I've shagged top class hookers. I've been to Amsterdam and stayed in posh hotels. I've been in jails all over the place. I've met mass murderers and serial

killers.' The lad gave an impressive pause. 'I've even met Curtis Warren,' he

announced in the same tone of voice in which a saintly, old priest might declare,

'I have met the Pope.'

I turned to the second lad. 'What exactly have you done?' I inquired.

The lad spoke up. 'I've been to Ibiza,' he replied triumphantly.

We all burst out laughing and both young men looked highly indignant.

The second lad turned towards me and the two officers. 'Have you ever done

anything as exciting and as interesting as we have Boss?' he asked curiously.

'I've been all over Europe twenty times,' one prison officer commented.

The second screw also spoke up. 'I was in the army before I was a screw,' he

declared. 'I travelled the world. I saw active service in Northern Ireland, the

Middle East. Afghanistan.'

The second lad spoke again, this time to me. 'How about you, Boss?' he asked

politely. 'Have you ever been abroad?"

I thought for one long moment. I remembered some of the high tides of my life.

The winter of 2004 when I shot a 300lb deer in the Rockie Mountains......sailing

across the Caribbean in a catamaran…. sailing across the Gulf of China in a

dhow……Paris, Rome, Cape Town, Istanbul, New Orleans, Singapore, Hong

Kong, Buenos Aires, Bangkok, Zanzibar, Mombasa. The stone city of Petra, the ruins of Carthage.

And many other places.

Both screws and cons were waiting for me to speak. I felt as if I ought to say

something so finally, I spoke up.

'I once drove right across Africa from the west coast to the east coast and back,'

I explained mildly. 'It was a great trip.'

'Ah yes!' the first lad expostulated triumphantly. 'But there are no birds and no

nightclubs in Africa are there Boss?'

I had no answer to that.

Though personally I can't stand nightclubs!

A SAD STORY.

I once met two boys who had just been sentenced to thirty-two and thirty-five years each, recommended minimum. Apparently, they were paid as contract-

hire killers to murder some unlucky man. They shot this unfortunate person

eight times. They were paid six thousand pounds for doing this.

One of them boasted. 'My girl is sticking by me Boss.'

I did not say anything. I just had a moment's mental glimpse of some teenage

girl waiting over thirty years for a lad who she hardly knew. It didn't seem a

very likely scenario but as I reasoned to myself. 'They have both had a rather

bad day why make it worse?'

'Are you sorry for what you did?' I asked.

'I'll tell you what Boss,' one of them bragged. 'You don't make money like

that.'

I got my calculator out and did some simple maths. Six thousand pounds cash

divided by sixty-seven years worked out at eighty-nine pounds sterling per year.

Again, eighty-nine pounds divided by the 365 days of the year works out at .24

of a penny per day. Just short of a quarter of a penny per day. In the old days we

used to call that a farthing. A shilling was twelve pennies or in our money

nowadays five pence. Half a penny was a halfpenny and half a halfpenny was a

farthing. I looked at these boys and remembered just how many middle-aged

men I have interviewed who would sit and talk to me sadly and state. 'I have

wasted my life Boss. I have spent twenty, thirty or forty years in and out of jail.

I could have made more money working in a factory.'

One simple truth that prison teaches you repeatedly is that life is what you make

it. You never get a second bite at the cherry. If you mess up, then you are

lumbered with that result. Forever!

And, 'Forever is a very long time.'

(Funnily enough I once wrote a book with that title. Published by Amazon.)

One of the boys grinned again. 'Maybe we are in jail, but you don't make

money like that do you?' he repeated.

'You are right,' I admitted. 'I don't make anything like that kind of money.'

I paused and looked seriously at these two eighteen years old lads who had

ruined their own lives as well as the life of the man they had murdered and his

friends and family as well.

'You have got an awful long time to come to terms with what happened today,'

I explained to them. So just take it easy. It will be difficult at first, but as time

passes it will get easier.' I paused. 'But tell me something,' I requested again

with genuine curiosity. 'Do either of you feel sorry for that man whom you

shot? I mean he had never harmed either of you in anyway.'

'It was just business Boss,' one of them replied. 'Nothing personal.' They had

obviously either seen, 'the Godfather, 'film, or read the book, or more likely,

spoken to someone who had.

I think I was supposed to be impressed.

Incredibly enough though I felt quite sorry for them.

A farthing a day!

Mind you I felt even more sorry for the innocent man whom they had

murdered.

AN EXTREMELY UNPLEASNT INMATE.

Sometimes in jail you meet a man who looks just like the popular conception of

what a criminal is supposed to look like. This new man was transferred in from

another prison. He sat there and laughed in my face. He was a big, fat, smelly,

uncouth, unwashed object who seemed to find the entire situation hilarious.

When I admitted him there was a large colour photograph of him pinned onto

the front of his file. In this photo his face was bloody and battered and he looked as if he had been dragged through the proverbial hedge backwards. I

pointed to this photograph.

'What happened there?' I asked curiously.

The man's face was now completely clean and clear of bruises.

'I indecently assaulted a female officer in my last prison,' he boasted. 'The

screws there twisted me up and gave me a good hiding.' He laughed again. 'I've

been to court today and I got seven years for the assault.'

It is custom and practice in the Prison Service that if an inmate attacks a staff

member in a prison then he is transferred to another prison afterwards.

I kept my own face expressionless. 'How do you feel about the seven years?'

I asked him in a deadpan voice.

The man laughed again. 'Fuck it!' he laughed. 'It was worth it.'

I finished the paperwork and shoved the appropriate forms across the desk at

him. 'Sign there and there,' I ordered. 'And then get out of my sight.'

He looked surprised and indignant, but he signed and then walked out.

I never saw him again.

I completed an SIR form stating that in my opinion he was extremely dangerous

to female staff and that in no circumstances should he be left alone with any

female.

THE LITTLE GIRL.

A new man came into the prison. He was a staunch supporter of animal rights and was also a believer in non-violence towards animals. Consequently, he

started sending letter bombs to butchers, gamekeepers and other 'war criminals'

that he and his friends disliked. One letter was opened by a little girl, the

daughter of the intended recipient and she was badly injured. I asked him how

he felt about this and his reaction was an indifferent shrug. 'There is a war on,'

he replied. 'People get killed and injured in wars.'

What a great answer I thought. 'A man opposed to violence who is prepared to

main and mutilate to achieve his aims.' A pacifist, anti-hunting, anti-shooting,

anti-fishing vegetarian who says he is opposed to cruelty. In prison you meet

every conceivable different type of person and you quickly learn to be tolerant.

If you don't then you will not last in the job. It is as simple as that. Sometimes

you meet people who you click with and feel an affinity to. Other times you

meet people whom you dislike. 'If I were you, I would be careful of letting the

ordinary lads know what you are in for,' I advised.

He looked at me in surprise. 'What do you mean?' he asked.

'In jail anything to do with hurting children is a sensitive issue,' I explained.

'Just be careful of what you say and who you say it to.'

'I'm not ashamed of anything I've done,' he expostulated indignantly. 'I am

fighting to save this planet. I am an eco-warrior.'

Apparently, this man went onto an ordinary Wing and lost no time in telling the other inmates that he was 'a prisoner of conscience,' and that he had been jailed

for his beliefs. This was an abuse of his human rights because he was a

'prisoner of war' and should be treated as such. People who are fanatics often

have difficulty in realising that most other people do not agree with them. With

this animal rights man this was the situation was identical. Several ordinary

inmates had severe words with him, but he was adamant and repeated that he

had done 'nothing to be ashamed of.' Several of the hard cases on the wing approached an officer and told him in no

uncertain terms that that this man was going to be severely assaulted. The

officer told them 'leave it with me. I will deal with it.' The officer did.

So, the man ended up being transferred to the VP Wing anyway.

He was very indignant about this.

THE SELF HARMER.

This man was an interesting case. When I met him, he was in his mid-thirties

and he had a history of self-harm which went back to when he was a child. This

man was probably the worst self-harmer I ever met in my entire life. He

regularly slashed his own arms, legs, wrists and body. The slashes on his left

arm was so bad that it was impossible to stitch them up anymore. He came

from a badly dysfunctional background and he had spent a lifetime in foster

homes, youth custody centres of all kinds, Borstals, detention centres and prisons. He abused and used alcohol and every variety of drugs, legal and illegal

on a daily, in fact hourly basis. When you meet such people whether as patients

in a Mental Health Hospital or as inmates in prisons the one fact that astounds

you are the fact that they are still alive. The reasons are obvious. Once they are

dead you no longer meet them. Except perhaps, once in a blue moon, on a

mortuary slab or hanging from a noose in a jail cell. People like this have low

self-esteem. Many of them have told me quite seriously that when they slash

themselves it gives them a real thrill. Apparently, some chemical is released into

the body in these situations. I suppose if you have got nothing better to do then

it beats staring at brick walls. Though, personally, I have to say, I would rather stare at brick walls. For some reason, probably because no one else wanted the

job, I was asked to be his 'key worker.' This simply meant that I was supposed

to visit the man whenever I had any free time and try and build up some

meaningful relationship during which he would come to accept my advice and

would try and find alternative coping strategies rather than in self-harming.

One problem with this was that I very seldom had any free time. I was usually

frantically busy. Most of the female staff who I worked with were great. But a

significant minority displayed the tactics which I suffered during the eighteen

months of torture of my R.G.N. training course when I was surrounded by

petty-minded individuals who could not understand what psychiatry is and whose definition of 'work' was running around 'looking busy.' Many of the so-

called trained staff of those days would regard it as their duty 'to keep the

students busy.' So instead of talking to some poor old man who was dying and

who desperately wanted someone to talk with you would be told, 'go and clean

the sluice out,' or 'tidy the linen room.'

To be fair most of the RGN girls in Altcourse were far more mature than that.

But there was still the under-laying stratum of idiocy in which people totally

lose sight of important matters and rave about petty, trivial affairs which are not

in the slightest bit important.

Nevertheless, I still managed to see my friend quite a lot and we had some good

chats.

I visited him on one occasion in his pad when I had a student with me. He made

me welcome and showed me the latest additions to his collection of dirty

magazines. Then he asked me if I would like a cup of coffee. I accepted and he

made me a cup with his little kettle. He used his own powdered milk and coffee.

We chatted freely for half an hour.

As we were walking back to the Hospital Unit the student asked me questions.

She did not like the fact that I had looked at his dirty magazines. She felt that

these were demeaning to women. She was also puzzled as to why I had

accepted a coffee when I had specifically warned her against doing this. They

were serious questions. I gave her serious answers.

'This man was making me welcome,' I explained. 'He has spent a lifetime in

custody of one form or another. The only way he can make us welcome is to

show me his latest dirty magazines and he has just given me a cup of his own

coffee. In jail the opportunity for an inmate to show friendship to a member of

staff is very limited. In fact, almost impossible. But he is doing the best he can.

What am I supposed to do in return?"

To be fair this student seemed to accept the point I was making.

When I last saw this man, he was spending his time touring around prisons and

Mental Health Hospitals and giving talks on self-harm to assorted audiences of

staff and patients. Apparently, he really enjoyed doing this and he was fluent and convincing. He was a great success. I like to think that he was another of

my very small success stories.

If you ever read this my old friend (J.K.) then, from your old mate Chris, all the

best. And take care of your kids.

THE DIRTY PROTEST.

I walked into the Segregation Unit one day. 'We've got a right one here Chris,'

the big, well-built prison officer announced as I entered.

'What's the problem?' I asked.

The officer indicated a pair of solid, wooden doors which I thought were a large

cupboard. From somewhere nearby I could vaguely hear muffled chanting and shouting from which sounded like some form of weird religious intonation. The

officer unlocked the door and showed me the strip cell.

This was, 'the bottom line,' in Altcourse Jail. It was simply a bare, barren cell

with walls of rough concrete. There was a single plastic chamber pot. The

window was a single, heavily barred aperture set high up and well out of reach.

It consisted of frosted glass covered in steel bars. This cell was reserved for the

most troublesome of inmates.

At that moment it was inhabited by one peculiar fellow. He was a tall, lean,

dirty, dishevelled young man who was stark naked apart from streaks of shit all

over his body and a few tattered scraps of what had obviously been clothing.

People in such cells are issued with a one-piece smock which is, supposedly

tear-proof. The mattress is made of similar, very tough material and is also

supposed to be tear resistant as well. I am here to tell you that these materials

are most certainly not tear-proof. The lad was jumping up and down while at the

same time carrying out a non-stop song and dance act with incredible energy.

The whole cell reeked of human faeces and urine. The floor and ceilings were

streaked with ornate lines of human shit. Pools of water and urine littered the

landscape. Bits of food were scattered haphazardly around the floor and stuck to

the walls. The man had ripped his own mattress into pieces which must have

taken an awful lot of energy. Apparently, he had used his teeth to do this. He must have had one remarkably strong pair of gnashers. The cell looked and

stank like the lair of some prehistoric, semi-human, Neanderthal monster. Even

from outside of the cell the stench was appalling.

I am not giving to swearing but I regarded the man and turned to the screw.

'Jesus Christ!' I ejaculated. 'How long has this been going on for?'

'He's been carrying on like this for the last four days,' the screw explained

with a grin. 'And this pantomime has been going on non-stop ever since he was

admitted.'

I have witnessed this behaviour pattern before. It is a recognised, albeit very

unusual, personality trait. If you make yourself stay awake long enough then after three or four days without sleep you will start hallucinating and become

high. If you simply couldn't care less about yourself or anyone else, then it is a

fool proof way of causing trouble to yourself and staff. Most people in jail want

to get out. This man was obviously just enjoying himself.

Surprisingly enough he was NOT a person with any kind of recognised

grievance against the system. He was not demonstrating against the police, the

prison service or any individual judge, lawyer or other official. He was not

claiming to be innocent. He was just a man, who came into prison with the

declared intention of being as difficult as possible and causing as much trouble

as possible. And, of course he was not prejudiced. He did not care in the slightest who he caused trouble too. He made trouble for prisoners, trusties,

screws, nurses, doctors. Anyone would do. The officers nudged each other

and wandered off to see to the remainder of their motley crew.

The prisoner smiled into my face in a friendly manner and then squatted down

and defecated. I got ready to duck in case he suddenly hurled a lump of shit

at me but I need not have worried. He rummaged through the stinking pile of

human faeces until he found the object of his search. He did not shout out with

glee. He just gave a huge grin of satisfaction.

I turned and called for a prison officer. I surmised that he had recovered a

balloon or condom full of drugs and he wanted to swallow them as quickly as possible before he was twisted up and the drugs were confiscated. The man

skilfully but carefully opened the balloon and quickly extracted one tablet. With

a huge grin on his face he quickly swallowed the pill and, just as quickly he

knotted the balloon again and just as quickly swallowed it.

The balloon was still coated in the human shit which had been coated it on its'

passage through this man's bowels and rectum but this did not seem to

bother him in the least.

When I informed the screws of this development, they simply gave wry grins.

'We know he has that package plugged inside himself,' they explained. 'But he

usually waits until there is no-one around before he pulls that stunt.'

'He came in with that packet inside himself,' another officer explained. 'He

defecates it out every day or so and then swallows a tablet. We reckon he has

about twenty tablets in the pack. He has used four so five so far. The remainder

should keep him as high as a kite for the rest of his stretch. He is swallowing

either speed or acid.'

(SPEED; shorthand for amphetamines; illegal drugs which are stimulants which

get a person high.

ACID; shorthand for Lysergic Dythalidamide which is a mind-bending,

hallucinatory drug. A tiny capsule or tablet the size of a pin head can cause a

'trip,' lasting fourteen or fifteen hours during which a person will experience

hallucinations, delusions and the other experiences of a florid, psychotic state of schizoid insanity.)

'If he goes on swallowing shit then he will get an infection of some kind or another,' I pointed out.

The screw shrugged his shoulders. 'He has been told that,' he explained. 'Lots of times. By both nurses and by doctors. His answer was, 'I couldn't care less.'

Many inmates prefer this state to being in a conscious, aware, awake state of normality. Prison is very boring. I have never tried these substances, but many prisoners assure that it is a great way to do your time.

I will take their word for it.

Before this man was discharged, he ran out of illegal tablets and calmed down somewhat.

I was quite interested in this case, so I paid him a few more visits. When I

talked seriously to him on a one to one basis I asked him exactly why he was

behaving in this way. All I got was a load of facetious rubbish.

In the 1960's when hallucogenic drugs were the height of fashion the Hippies of

that era had a very expressive description which portrayed the drug users of that

time. They used to say. 'He went on a trip and he never came back.'

Drugs such as this induce temporary insanity. In big doses over a long period of

time they induce permanent insanity. But people like the man I have just

described enjoy the experience of being insane. Prison staff used to ask me in

all seriousness.

'Can't we send him to a psychiatric hospital?

'Can't we get this man some treatment?'

The answer is depressing and boringly bad.

No! You cannot treat people who do not want to be treated.

On a final note I should point out that this man's outrageous behaviour did not

affect the prison staff in the least. To say that Prison Staff are broad minded is

the understatement of the year. All he achieved was mild amusement. Every

couple of days he would be ordered into a fresh cell. If he refused, then three

screws in overalls would twist him up and take great pleasure in lifting him to

a nearby cell. Then a couple of trusties would take a fire hose into the dirty cell and wash down the muck and clean the cell out. This would take perhaps half an

hour after which silly boy would promptly be replaced back into his original

home.

The trusties were paid for this. They didn't care.

The screws were paid. They didn't care.

I was paid as well. I didn't care.

All in all, a rather pointless exercise.

And before anyone protests at these heartless, cynical attitudes of prison staff let

me just say. 'If caring made any difference then I would care.'

A very old prison saying.

A DRINK OF WATER.

When you meet a man or men who are convicted, or even accused, of sexual

offences against small children it is sometimes difficult to keep your humanity

intact. But I always remind myself of stories such as the treatment of the

Birmingham Six and other innocent men whose claims of innocence were

greeted with roars of laughter. Many years later they were proved to be

innocent. Other than in being in the wrong place at the wrong time.

And some inmates turn your stomach with accounts of sexual misconduct with

babies, their mothers, fathers and other disgusting tales. But you must always

remember the golden rule.

'You are a volunteer. Not a conscript. However distasteful you find a person.

Just remember. You are being paid money to do a job. So! Just do the job.'

An old man limped painfully into my office and explained that he had been

transferred from a prison 'down South.' He had been travelling in the sweat box

for the entire day. He was serving a long sentence for sexual offences against

small children.

'Excuse me Boss,' he asked politely in a well-educated voice. 'Could I have a

drink of water please? I started my journey ten hours ago and I am very thirsty.'

I thought for a moment and then gestured to the sink in the corner. 'Help

yourself,' I instructed him. There were lots of little medicine cups there and the

old man washed one out and then drained it a dozen times while I started on the paperwork. He obviously was very thirsty. A prison officer walked in and

glared nastily both at me and the new inmate. 'Alright fellah!' he announced.

'You are going on the VP wing.' Officers in Altcourse usually called inmates,

'Mr Smith,' or 'Mr Jones,' or whatever, although many inmates preferred to be

called by their first names. The term 'fellah' was reserved for unpopular clients.

The officer glared at me as well. I ignored the officer and continued completing

the paperwork.

Later that day the same officer approached me. 'Why did you give that swine

water?' he asked. 'He's a nonce. He's a kiddy fiddler.'

I thought carefully again and finally spoke. 'I have no sympathy or brief for child molesters,' I explained slowly. 'But I am paid money to do a job and that

old man asked me for a drink of water. I gave him a drink of water.'

Again, the officer glared at me and then stormed out of the room and slammed

the door loudly.

I suppose you could debate this issue endlessly.

Much as I dislike and detest child molesters.

On balance I think I was right.

You could write a book about it.

FOUR MILLION POUNDS.

A man walked into Admissions and sat down quite calmly. 'Been in jail

before?" I inquired.

'Oh yes Boss,' the man replied.

'What are you in for?' I asked.

'Just a bit of drugs Boss,' he replied politely.

'Smack? Crack? Grass? Whizz?' I asked

'Just a bit of grass Boss,' he answered. 'Just for my personal use.'

'Really. How much,' I asked.

The man looked at me narrowly. 'Well,' he replied slowly. 'Apparently the

street value was four million pounds.'

I burst out laughing.

BURIED BODIES!

Due to the nature of the job which I did I probably put in more S.I.R.s than just

about anyone else. Every so often something happens in jail which, deliberately

or accidently, consciously or unconsciously, is rather funny.

One day I was sitting chatting in an informal manner with an inmate. The twin

subjects of murder and the disposal of dead bodies came up in the conversation.

As I have explained inmates in jail usually talk about crime and criminals. What

else can they talk about? After all many of them have spent most of their lives

in jail. To many members of the public jail is just like a foreign country and if

someone spent thirty years living in Mongolia or Kazakhstan then it would be

amazing if these countries did not figure in their conversations.

Quite casually this man told me how he had murdered several people and buried

their bodies in various fields out in the country. He described, in detail exactly

how he had murdered these people and where he had buried them. This was something that I simply could not ignore. I was somewhat dubious as to the

story's authenticity. Nevertheless, I duly completed an SIR and submitted it.

Sometimes when you took the time and trouble to do this the result is a

resounding silence.

On other occasions you might well get a polite letter thanking you. Sometimes

you might be interviewed by the police or the Prison Security Staff. In one

instance I ended up in Caernarvon Crown Court giving evidence at a murder

trial. Most times there is no response at all. On this occasion though, in casual

conversation, one of the Security Staff informed me that numerous police

officers had been employed in digging these fields and other nearby fields looking for dead bodies. Even modern sophisticated scanning devices had been

used to see if there were bodies buried there. Nothing at all had been found.

A few weeks later the same man approached me on the wing and chatted

cheerfully. 'Did the police dig those fields up Boss?' he inquired.

I played dumb. Not difficult for me. 'I don't know,' I replied casually.

The man laughed. 'I had a visit the other day from my mate. He lives near those

fields. He said the area had been swarming with coppers, but they found

nothing.'

'Well why did you say there were dead bodies there?' I asked.

The man grinned. 'I dunno Boss,' he answered. Then he grinned again with a certain tatty charm. 'To be honest it just seemed like a good idea. You see I

owed that farmer a few favours and I knew he needed his fields digging over.'

A RATHER UNUSUAL PROTEST.

On one particularly dark and dirty evening while I was making my way across

the prison courtyards I became aware of a strange happening. Strange

happenings abound in prisons. The interiors of modern prisons are split up by

high wire fences are pierced at regular intervals by turnstiles which allow

inmates, access and egress. In the event of a riot or disturbance the Control

Officer can bang a button which automatically seals off any or all of these turnstiles. Staff have keys so are immune to such lock downs.

To get through a turnstile a prisoner must press a button, identify himself then

give his name and number. Each turnstile is contained inside a wire cage which

is itself surmounted by another wire fence. In effect each turnstile itself is

topped with an open, wire cage. In theory it is impossible to scale such an

obstacle. These are sheer wire fences with no grip or protuberances whatever.

As I walked across the courtyard, I saw to my surprise that a young inmate had

successfully climbed into the cage and was ensconced safely on top of the

turnstile. How on earth an inmate did manage this I simply cannot begin to

imagine but, as an eyewitness I am here to tell you that this lad actually did achieve this. I heard it said time and again in jails all over. 'If the inmates

put as much effort and energy into leading normal lives as they put into being

criminals they would be huge success.'

One of the Prison Managers was trying to have a serious conversation with this

inmate.

'Can I help?' I asked the Manager innocently as the young inmate continued

with his foul language and his protest. At least this is a bit more original than a

food refusal (hunger strike) or a dirty protest. (an inmate shits up, i.e. he covers

his body in human shit.)' I thought to myself.

The Manager took me to one side and spoke to me quietly. 'You are trained in

psychiatry,' he expostulated. 'For Christ's sake how can we get him to come down.' I could appreciate the problem. To get a First Response Team up this

wire fence would be difficult to say the least. If not impossible. And, if this silly

boy continued with his protest then the on-going protest would be disruptive as

well. But something had to be done. The situation could not be allowed to

continue. The longest roof-top protest in British Prison history lasted a year and

a half. (Yes, that's right! A YEAR AND A HALF!)

I seriously considered the situation for a minute or so. One of the constant, on-

going problems which, I encountered in psychiatry, particularly in prisons is

events like this. Ordinary people expect you to be able to wave a magic wand

and solve a problem which in fact is absolutely nothing to do with psychiatry.

Psychiatry is the treatment of a mental illness. I turned to the Manger.

'It is getting cold,' I pointed out. 'And it is going to start raining soon.'

'So!' he asked tersely. 'Who cares?'

'Well why don't you turn the fire hose on him,' I suggested. 'If he is soaking

wet and freezing cold that will bring him down quicker than anything else I can

imagine.'

The Manager stared at me in sheer horror. On calm reflexion many years later, I

can't say that I blame him. Prisons are always terrified of bad publicity. And a

story like that could easily make terrible, newspaper headlines.

They did not turn a fire hose on him. The man eventually simply got bored and

came down of his own accord.

The New York Police have a very calm and well understood philosophy when

dealing with any kind of hostage situation or stand-off of this kind.

Their philosophy is, 'we bore them to death.' This is not nearly as dramatic as

bursting through the doors or windows with guns blazing. However, it is

probably a better solution than violence and mayhem.

On reflection I would say that the Manger was right.

And I was wrong.

Violence should always be a last option rather than a first option.

At times in British Prisons, you feel like losing your temper.

Losing your temper is never a good idea.

'YOU CAN'T TAKE THIS OFF ME.'

Drug addiction causes endless problems in every facet of society but in prisons

the problems are exacerbated to the extreme. A man came into a jail after being

arrested for possession of illegal drugs. They were a large quantity of

amphetamines. More commonly known as Speed this is a drug which causes all

sorts of problems in jail. Many people who abuse speed become aggressive in

personality. This man was aggressive anyway.

I completed the usual procedures and he signed the appropriate forms.

'Alright you are finished,' I told him. 'Send the next man in.'

The fellow looked at me indignantly. 'I want my speed,' he snarled aggressively. Apparently when arrested the police took a large quantity of

chemical substances off this man. He had been remanded in custody and his

property had been sent to the prisons with him.

It was his property. He wanted it.

'When you are discharged from this prison you can ask for it back,' I explained

patiently. 'You don't really think that you are going to be admitted to a Cat 'A'

jail and be allowed to keep a quantity of illegal drugs.'

'You are not a police officer,' the man snarled nastily. 'You have no legal right

to take that off me. I want my own property and I am not leaving this office

until I get it.'

I picked up my intercom and phoned the Admissions Manager.

And yes!

He did leave my office. With a bit of persuasion.

No!

He did not get his amphetamines.

One more example of stupid people who have totally unrealistic expectations.

RACIAL PREJUDICE IN PRISONS.

In the modern day and age in which we live most people are far less prejudiced

than during my own younger days. Many words which have unpleasant and/or

insulting connation are no longer freely used. In 2005 I gave evidence at

the Mubarek Inquiry which was the most high-profile inquiry the prison service has ever seen.

As a result of the horrible murder of a young Asian lad named Zahid Mubarek

by an unpleasant, young psychopath named Robert Stewart the whole concept

of cell-sharing was being seriously questioned.

Apparently, this white lad had been seen by a Mental Health Nurse who had

written in his medical file. 'In my opinion he has a long-standing, deep-seated

personality disorder.' And, 'he shows a glaring lack of remorse, feeling, insight

or any other emotion.'

The Mental Health Nurse in this instance was me.

(If you want to read a full account of this case read. 'My stretch in Altcourse

Prison,' by Chris Kinealy published on Amazon.)

Some years later the staff in Altcourse Prison, and other prisons were given a

document to read and to sign. The documents listed words which staff must

NOT use under any circumstances.

These words were Nigger, Paki, Coon, Wog and, surprisingly enough, the word

Negroe.

I was surprised at the inclusion of Negroe. As far as I am concerned this word is

simply an adjective which describes a man from Africa or of African descent.

In Altcourse we were all ordered to sign this document and we were all

informed that if we heard any of our colleagues using any of these words, we

should complete a Security Information Report and inform on them.

I thought that an S.I.R. was for matters of SECURITY.

How the hell this could be defined as a security issue is beyond me.

I personally felt that this was a massive example of overkill.

The problem with being politically correct is that someone keeps on changing

the rules. Not to mention creating new ones. And you are expected to keep

abreast of whatever the new politically correct term is even if no one tells you

what it is.

Some years ago, while working in Risley Prison I used the expression,

'coloured people.' I was sternly admonished and told NEVER to use this again.

The correct description is, 'black people' I was told in no uncertain terms.

I can put my hand on my heart and state, truthfully, that in all my years in lots of different prisons and police custody suites all round Britain not once ever did

I hear a prion officer racially insult any Black, Asian or Gay inmate ever.

METHADONE.

A PERSONAL OPINION!

Prior and during the Second World War the German Government, who knew

better than anyone that a war was coming took many precautions. Some of

these precautions were bizarre and evil in the extreme. Rounding up and

murdering thousands of people whom they disliked was one precaution.

One of their slightly more rational precautions was the invention of methadone.

In any war soldiers get wounded and there is a desperate need for pain killers.

The most powerful pain killer known is diamorphine, or to give it the slang term

heroin. Opium is obtained from poppies and when refined it becomes morphine

which is much stronger. Refined again it becomes heroin which is stronger

again. The Germans invented Methadone as a substitute for heroin. The poppy

which heroin is obtained from only grows in hot climates so, basically the Nazis

invented artificial heroin. It was named after ADOLF the slime who led the

Third Reich.

There is a huge difference between the muck that junkies buy on the street and

the carefully prepared British pharmaceutical drug which is legally prescribed

by doctors as an analgesic. This is usually only given such cases as terminal cancer.

It has happened that junkies sometimes obtain pure diamorphine when they

burgle chemists' shops or steal it from some other source. They cook up a fix

and it kills them. This is because they are so used to street muck which is

normally about ten per cent pure. The strength of the muck can be as low as one

percent. A useful side effect of this is that it is much easier to wean addicts of

the weak supply rather than the more powerful stuff.

Street heroin is heavily mixed with flour, sugar, brick dust or any rubbish. I

once met a junkie who injected heroin that turned out to be Vim the cleaning

powder. He did not get high on it!

Time and time again I have sat and listened to junkies who tell you that they desperately need to get of drugs and in the meantime, they want huge dosages

of medication to get them off drugs. This is simply rubbish. Giving drugs to

drug addicts is a complete and utter waste of time. Another complete and

utter fallacy is the terrible effects of 'withdrawal,' from heroin. Like most

normal people my experience of heroin addiction was minimal before I worked

in the Prison Service. Most of what we all know, or rather what we 'think we

know' comes from lurid novels and films in which the poor, deprived heroin

addict is given a shot of heroin by some devious, evil drug pusher and he is an

addicted slave ever afterwards.

Again, this is rubbish. Most people have little or no knowledge of withdrawal other than what the addict tells them. But the addict has a very strong reason for

telling lies. The addict hopes that when he ends up in court, he can convince the

judge or magistrate to be lenient with him because of the terrible suffering he

was enduring with his withdrawal. In the meantime, of course he wants

'medication' as treatment for his, 'illness.' His 'illness' is 'withdrawal.'

In fact, the famous 'rattle,' is no worse than a bad dose of the flu. Many an

addict has run out of money, or their supplier has been arrested or has been

unable to obtain drugs for whatever reason and has simply had to cope with

no drugs at all. So what? Withdrawal does not kill you. It is simply an

unpleasant experience. Drug addiction is self-induced anyway. But to become an addict in the first place the person has an addictive or weak personality. In

prisons doctors and Mental Health Nurses are faced with an endless parade of

people who demand painkillers, tranquilisers, sleeping tablets, anti-depressants

and an incredible litany of absolutely anything that they believe will give them a

high or a buzz of some form or another. I met men who claimed that they were

addicted to ketamine which is a horse tranquiliser. You would ask yourself in all

seriousness who the hell was the idiot who first decided to try this. The answer

is simple. There are men and women out there who will try absolutely anything.

The person will shrug his shoulders and state. 'Well! What the hell the worst it

can do is kill me. Who cares anyway?'

Of course, when arrested and they end up in 'police custody,' or jail the

situation is 'different,' and the man demands, 'treatment,' by which he

invariably means, 'medication,' or 'tablets.'

'Why do they want tablets?" you would ask.

The answer is depressingly simple. They would prefer heroin or cocaine. But

since that is not possible in jail they will lie, scheme, plot, plan and manipulate

to obtain something, anything else.

During my many years in jails I met literally thousands of people who claimed

to be suffering from withdrawal. I never met one single one of them who died as

a result.

PLUGGING.

This is a procedure which is commonly used in both female and male prisons

throughout the world. It simply consists of someone secreting objects inside

their rectum and/or vagina. In days gone by prison staff could carry out invasive

searches into these places but due to the human rights of prisoners this is no

longer permitted in Britain. Women have twice as many places to hide objects

so, it is far easier for them to smuggle than for men. It is truly amazing when

you see the size and dimensions of the objects which people have managed to

secrete inside themselves. But as the old saying goes. 'If you can get a baby's

head through it then you can get anything through it.'

A variation of this practice is when a person swallows a packet or object which will be defecated out in a day or so. An old lag who was frequently admitted to

Altcourse Jail was nicknamed 'the suitcase,' because he made a lot of money

smuggling drugs in for his fellow gangsters. When the security staff became

aware of this practice his next admission was to Strangeways. (aka HMP

Manchester nowadays) When I last heard of him, he was in serious trouble with

his criminal colleagues because he owed them the price of the last consignment.

Apparently, they were demanding full payment for the amount he owed them.

It is now far more difficult to smuggle drugs in this fashion. A modern piece of

equipment is the BOSS chair. (BOSS; Body Orifice Security Scanner.) This

looks just like a rather cumbersome armchair. It is an x-ray, a metal detector and body scanner all in one. Any inmate with an object plugged will be invited to

produce the package. If he refuses, then he is transferred to the Segregation

Unit where they can serve their time.

THE TELEPHONE CALL.

Every so often in jail you manage to do something to help an inmate in some

way or other and when the person remembers the matter and, perhaps weeks or

months later and thanks you it is quite surprising and even heart-warming. As I

have always said 'anyone can end up in jail.' When I started work in Her

Majesty's Establishment's I made myself a serious promise. I told myself that if

an inmate made me a request and it was a reasonable request made in a reasonable manner then, if I could, I would always find time to carry out the

request. I am proud to say that I always kept this promise. Well! Most of the

time.

I was once walking through the Admissions Unit when I happened to notice an

inmate who was sitting by himself and was obviously furiously angry. For some

reason or other I stopped and spoke to him. The man was being transferred to a

Birmingham prison that day. He had used up the last of his phone credits so

he could not tell his wife this and she was travelling, by public transport, from

Liverpool to visit him the next day. But now, apparently, some security problem

had cropped up, and his transfer had been cancelled. The man asked the prison officers to phone his wife, so she could cancel her trip, but they refused. So, his wife would be making a long, arduous, totally pointless and expensive two-hundred-mile round journey just to be told. 'Your husband is not here. He is still in Altcourse.'

I could well understand his anger. It is incidents like this that make prisoners hate staff and inevitably, as night follows day, violence will ensue. I decided to act. 'Give me your telephone number,' I requested. 'I will phone your wife and tell her.'

The man was quite amazed, but he gave me the number and when I got back to the Healthcare Unit, I rang the lady in question. She was very grateful but was also confused as to why a Mental Health Nurse was telling her rather than an officer. For obvious reasons I did not go into any details. I simply told her that I

was telling the truth and not to bother with her planned trip tomorrow. She

thanked me. As far as I was concerned that was the last of it.

MONTHS LATER.

I was walking through the prison when a man approached me. He reached out

and shook hands. 'Thanks very much for that Boss,' he expostulated politely.

By then I had totally forgotten the entire incident, but the inmate obviously had

not. He recalled the episode to me, and I remembered it immediately. He stood

there and faced me. 'I really appreciated that Boss,' he explained seriously.

'Thanks very much.'

'Well that is my good deed for the week,' I used to myself. 'In fact, it must be

my good deed for the year.'

THE TURNSTILE.

On another occasion the rain was pouring down in solid rods of water when a

very, large, black gentleman spoke to me. 'Could you do me a favour please

Boss,' he requested politely. 'I have been waiting at this turnstile for twenty

minutes and my wife is in the Visits Centre.'

Turnstiles are a vital part of prison security. They split any prison up into

manageable portions. In the event of a riot or disturbance an officer in Control

can slam his hand onto a button and jam all the gates and turnstiles. This stops inmates from joining in any riot or disturbance. They also allow the staff to

monitor exactly where each inmate is inside the prison. Inmates must press a

button to contact control then give their name and ID whereas staff have keys.

Yet for some reason we could let inmates through the gates unless there was a

'freeze all movement,' order in force. I could never understand this. I unlocked

the gate and the inmate turned to me again. 'Could you do me another favour

please?' he requested. 'I have been waiting twenty minutes to get through this

gate. Could you possibly let me through the next gate so that I can then go to the

Visits Hall?' I could well understand this man's position. When you are waiting

for a visit nothing is more annoying than to be stuck in this manner. It was about forty metres across the courtyard to the next gate. I walked across to the

next gate in the pouring rain and let him through. It made me about five minutes

late for my appointment with another prisoner. One thing that all prisoners have

in abundance though is time. It cost me nothing.

About a year later I met the same man and again he thanked me. Again, he

remembered the event. Funnily enough, so did I.

THE SHOOTING MAN.

Another routine day in Admissions seeing murderers, rapists and robbers.

Nothing special. I think it was only when I retired and started meeting normal people again that I realised what a strange life I had been leading for nearly four

decades.

A new man entered. He was a well-built, middle-aged guy with the pronounced

swagger of the old lag and the moment he greeted me I could tell that he, 'knew

the score.'

'Alright Boss,' he greeted me cheerfully. 'How are you? Business seems good

for you guys nowadays.'

I could not help but grin. 'What are you in for?' I inquired.

The man grinned back. 'Selling guns Boss,' he replied politely.

I have always been a shooting man so naturally I was interested. Some years

ago the British government, in a fit of more than usual idiocy, decided to ban handguns to make Britain a safer place. This was just after a particularly

horrible man murdered a group of innocent children in Dunblane in Scotland.

He legally owned four pistols. A general election was pending and Labour and

Conservatives appeared to be having a competition with each other to see who

could claim to be, 'toughest on crime.' John Major promised to abide by the

results of the Cullen Inquiry into these horrific murders but, as one would

expect he double-crossed the shooting community and strongly pushed for

handguns to be banned. Like all law-abiding shooters I sadly handed in my

treasured collection of handguns. This expensive farce cost hundreds of jobs,

millions of pounds of tax-payers money and achieved absolutely nothing positive. In fact since then armed crime with handguns has actually increased. A

couple of coppers in the Midlands who were convicted and jailed for selling

these confiscated guns back to their underworld friends might be able to explain

one particular, very good reason why this procedure did not work.

Naturally I was curious. 'What kind of guns are they?' I inquired.

The man grinned. 'Smith and Wesson .357 revolvers,' he explained cheerfully.

'Which one?' I asked curiously. 'The model 66?'

'Not these Boss,' the man elaborated. 'These are the new version. The 656.

They are all in stainless steel with four inch barrels, ideal for concealment.

Wooden grips so they don't get slimy and slippery with rain or sweat.

Illuminated foresight,' he grinned. 'And each one comes complete with a hundred rounds of ammunition. Real bargain. Right?'

I gave an appreciative nod.

The man looked at me narrowly. 'Do you want to buy one Boss?' he asked me politely.

Just for once I was actually taken aback I looked straight at him. 'I'm a screw,' I protested.

The man looked shocked and surprised. 'We're not prejudiced. We sell to anyone,' he fumbled in his pockets. 'Look here Boss, he continued. 'I'll give you my mate's telephone number. He'll fix you up. Four hundred pounds! Like a said! A bargain.'

It is not often that I am shocked but this chap certainly managed it.

I thought for a moment then spoke. 'I don't really want to buy someone else's

history of armed robbery and murder,' I pointed out mildly.

Again the old lag looked appalled.'

'We wouldn't do that to you Boss,' he protested. 'These guns are all brand new.

Still in the box. Not one of them has ever been fired. Not ever.'

When the man had gone, I thought carefully for a minute or two and then

completed and SIR which detailed everything that this man had said.'

POLICE STORY.

This is the story of an event which happened to me after I left the Prison Service and was working for the Police.

ONE BIG LAD!

With the growth of reality television many of the general public have now

witnessed first-hand, albeit from the security of their living rooms, the atrocious

behaviour which police and prison staff tolerate daily. This has been a huge and

unexpected bonus for such staff. As a result, members of the public are far more

ready to believe prison and police staff when they listen to situations being

described which are, quite literally, unbelievable.

When I was employed by Manchester Police, I wandered into a police station

late one night and the duty Inspector approached me. 'Can I have a word with you please,' he requested politely.

I could see straight away that some emergency or untoward occurrence was

taking place. I was expecting to find someone covered in blood or something

similar.

The Inspector escorted me a police cell. Inside there was a big, well-built young

man, who was obviously extremely angry. He was running the full length of the

cell and head butting the steel door with enormous force. And he was doing this

repeatedly, again and again. 'Jesus Christ,' I swore softly to myself. This was in

the days before every cell had television watching it.

The Inspector explained lucidly. Apparently like many people this man had

been arrested for some minor offence or other and was thought to be on a combination of cocaine and alcohol.

When I started psychiatry, people abused either alcohol or drugs. Very few

people abused both at the same time. Some people who were either alcoholics

or drug addicts would abuse the alternative substance when they could not

obtain their preferred substance.

But by this time the idea of abusing both substances was creeping into popular

culture.

People on cannabis usually just sit there giggling and are easily amused. The

effects are akin to alcohol. Heroin and opiates have been likened to having a

good sexual orgasm while hallucogenic drugs are frequently compared to

dreaming. However, when cocaine and alcohol are mixed together the result is horrendous.

There is an old expression, 'he was fighting mad.' The old Vikings or Norsemen are believed to have abused a combination of magic mushrooms mixed with mead and the result was exactly what I have just described. The man goes, 'fighting mad.' Quite literally he, 'sees red.'

That night I stood and watched in appalled amazement as this young man repeatedly head butted the steel door. The Inspector grimaced. 'What do you recommend?' he asked seriously.

In a situation like this your options are limited.

Option number one, most people would say, would be to send the man to hospital. But the police must be practical. Realistically to do this would entail putting this man into a police wagon and physically carrying him into an 'A and

E unit'. To do this would take a minimum of at least four trained police staff,

probably a lot more. Staff who are desperately needed elsewhere for other

emergencies.

An Emergency Unit will be full of sick people who are waiting to see a doctor.

Imagine the fracas which would ensue if such a man was physically carried into

a hospital unit. Once there we would ask a doctor to see him. For what? To give

him treatment? What treatment? Possibly if he was being held down it might be

possible to give him an intra-venous injection. Providing that a doctor can be

found who is prepared to prescribe and then administer such an injection. But very few doctors would do this. For simple practical reasons. You have no

knowledge whatever what kind of pills, tablets or assorted muck the man might

already have swallowed, snorted or injected. These might well be contra-

indicated with any possible sedative. That is why when people are brought into

custody there is a standing rule that they are given nothing for the first six

hours. There is also the legal situation in cases like this. You cannot force

medication on a person against their will. Even in psychiatric hospitals such

measures can only be used in certain circumstances such as on a violent,

sectioned patient.

And if any reader is going to tell me. 'That is ridiculous,' then I can only reply.

'I completely agree with you.' But nevertheless, that is the law.

The Inspector gestured to the man who was still head butting the door. 'What do you recommend?' he asked calmly.

I thought for a moment and then suggested that I made a detailed written statement that I had personally witnessed this extreme behaviour and explain the incredible difficulty of giving any kind of medical treatment in these circumstances.

When I went into work over the next few days, I was expecting to get a message telling me that this man was dead, or brain damaged and that the C.I.D. wanted to interview me. Nothing of the sort happened.

As far as I know nothing happened the man.

Apparently, he went home the next day without a care in the world.

But I don't think it did his brain any good.

CONCLUSION.

I commenced psychiatry on the 4th January 1977. I was then twenty-five years

old. In 2015 I wrote to the Nursing and Midwifery Council and instructed them

to remove my name from the Nursing Register. By then I was sixty-three and I

really think that I had enough. To say that I was emotionally drained is the understatement of the year.

I once wrote a book, at the end of which, a couple of prison rioters had just been

sentenced to a recommended minimum of forty-five years each.

(The Book They Tried to Ban,' published by Amazon.)

I attached a poem about the prisoners who had just been sentenced to this

very, long stretch.

Well! I didn't quite make forty-five years.

But I managed thirty-eight years.

Do I have any regrets? No!

Not really.

BUT THIRTY-EIGHT YEARS BOY.

IS A VERY LONG TIME!

My next book is due out soon!

Printed in Poland
by Amazon Fulfillment
Poland Sp. z o.o., Wrocław